The Elements
FIRE

JUSTYN TIME

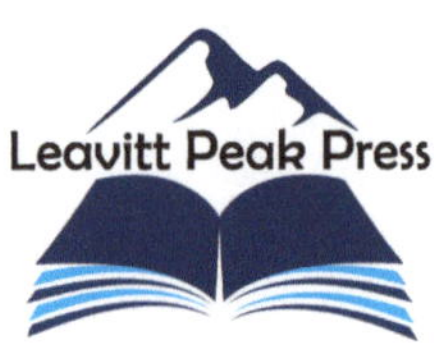

ISBN: 978-1-962363-37-2 (sc)
ISBN: 978-1-962363-38-9 (e)

Rev. date: 12/07/2023

Introduction

The five Elements are the Aether, Air, Earth, Fire and Water. Of these five elements, four are physical and the fifth, aether, is referred to as spiritual. It is the authors opiniion that they are all controlled by God, Jesus or you might call it Source or Universe. This thought process is predicated upon the theory that all of the elements have patterns within themselves. Patterns that when observed closely can be documented photographically. However, God can hide it all in plain site unless He decides to open your eyes. This book series Justyn Time, The Elements, showcases the patterns and designs within each of them. Justyn, challenges you to study the images, stare at them for 33 seconds and watch them come to life right before your eyes. We triple dog dare you to step into the magical realm that lies within each of the Elements.

Fire is closely linked to air. Fire needs three things in order to exist, oxygen Fuel and heat. The intensity of a fire varies because it is dependent upon the oxygen, fuel and heat available to it. A controlled fire can be used to illuminate a room or a house cook or barbecue food. It can also be photographed similar to how Justin has done while living with his good friend Hans Schmitt. He is the owner of Dance Boulevard in San Jose California and a Champion Dancer. They would sit on the back patio, enjoy food, drink and discuss all matters of life and existence.

During one such evening Justyn felt the spirit beckoning him to photograph the flamesof the firepit. In so doing he found that the flames would move in patterns almost as if dancing before his camera. He has captured over 20,000 fire images to date. Please note that the fire images have not been enhanced or photoshopped in any way. Some of the images may have been cropped to remove the black and negative space but the flames themselves have not been enhanced. As with the other elements each viewer sees the images from their own personal life perspective. What you see is what you see. Which is ultimately captivating and fascinating, we look forward to discovering what you see in the fire.

SERPENT

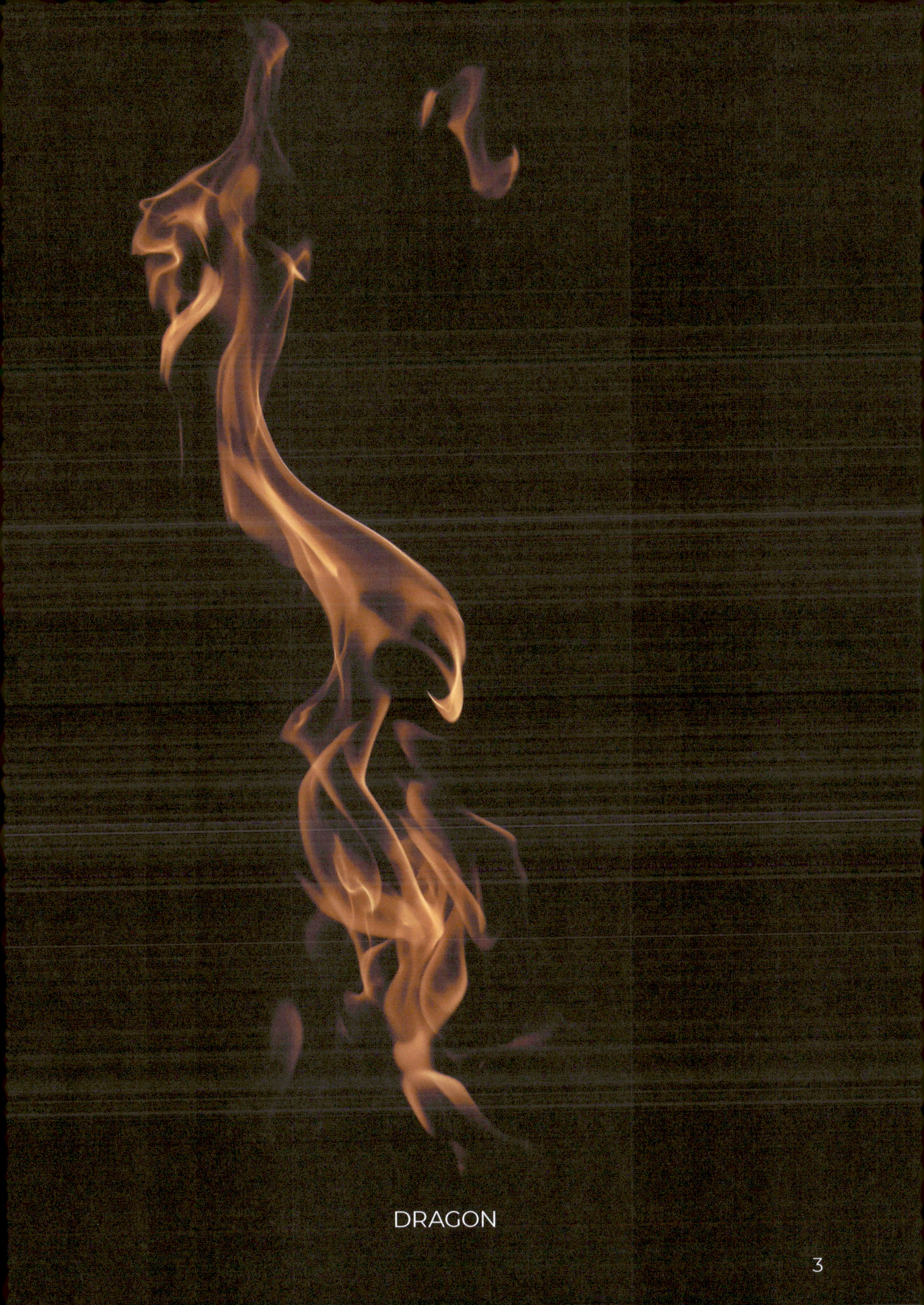

DRAGON

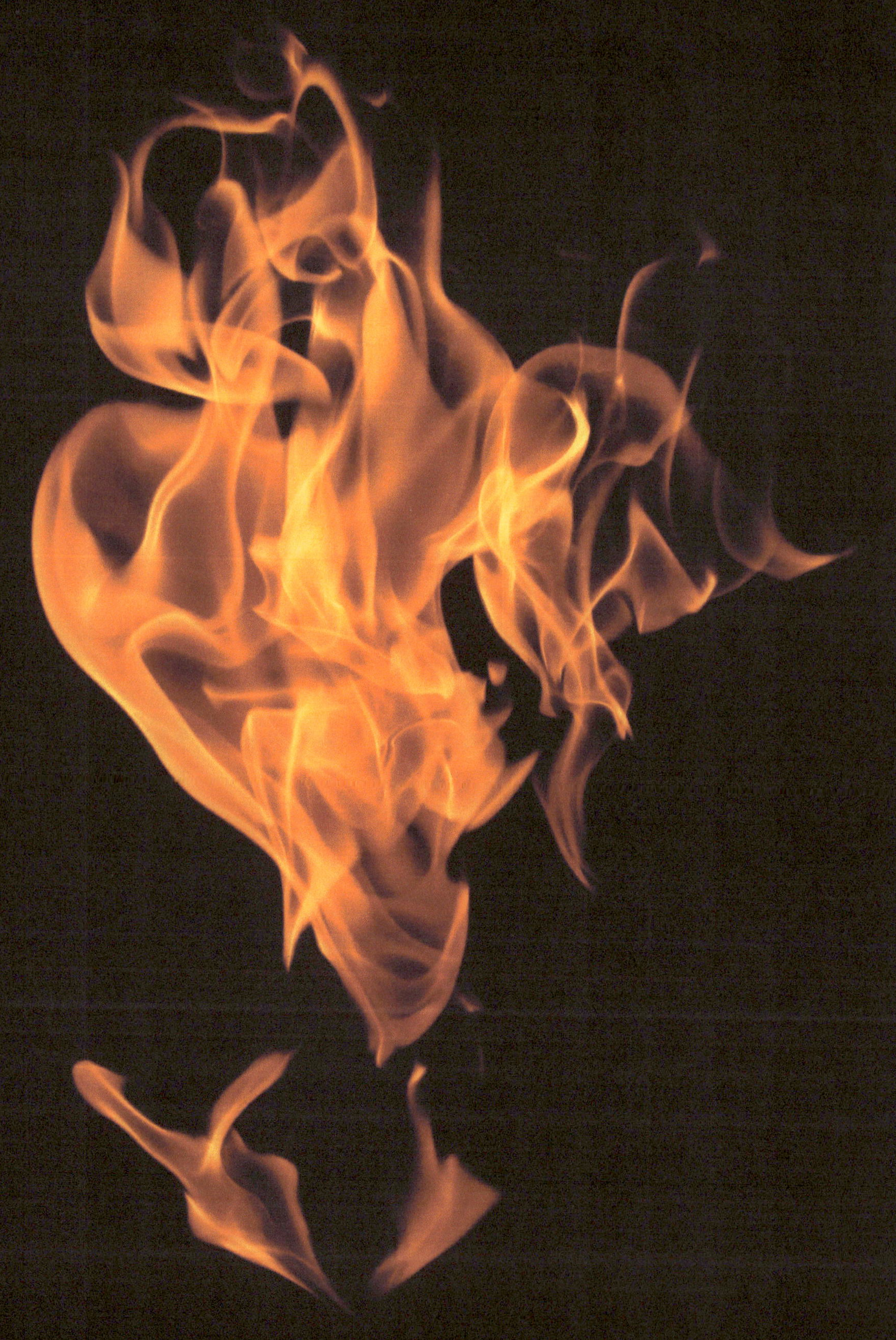

HEART ON FIRE

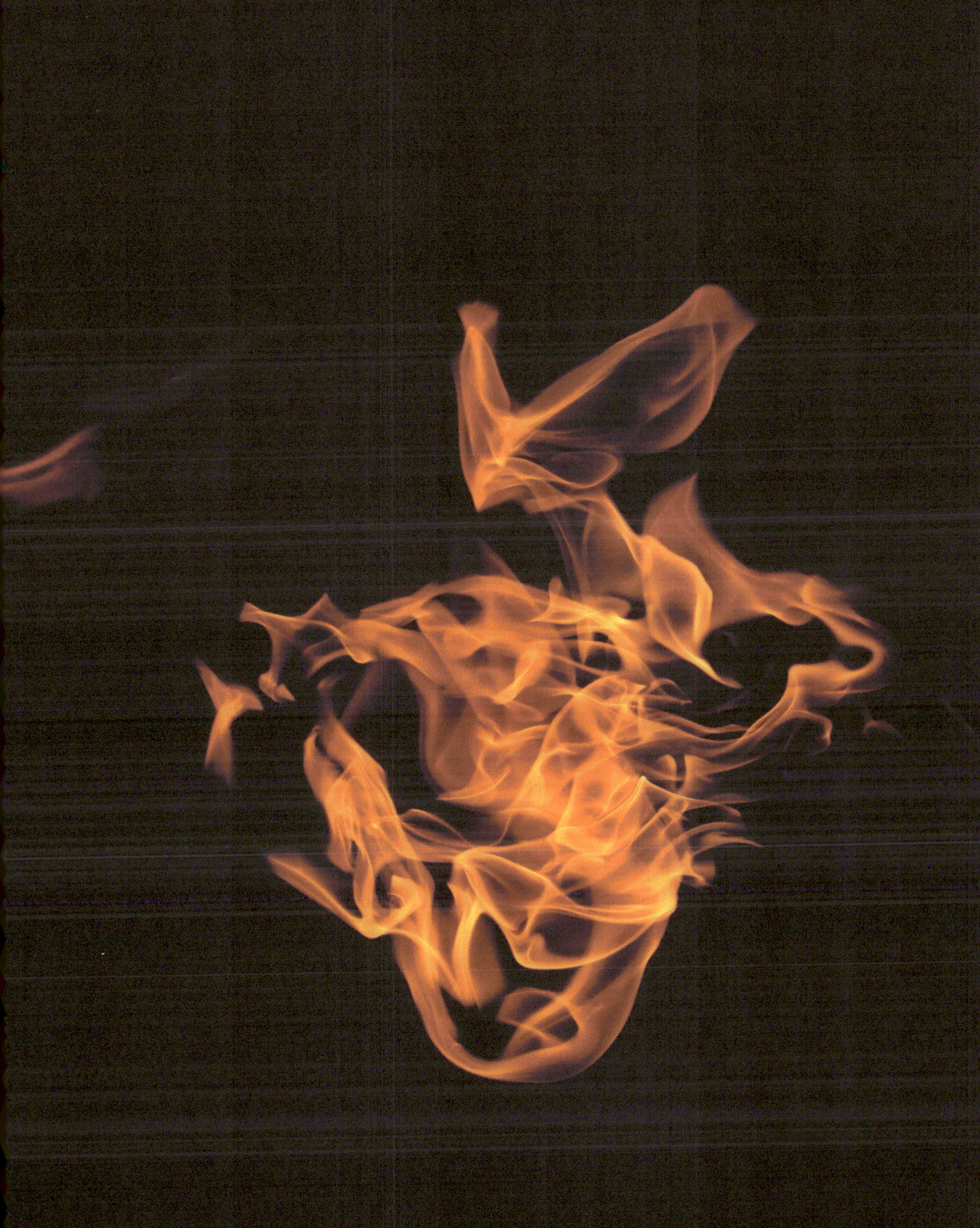

CONDORS BIRD NEST

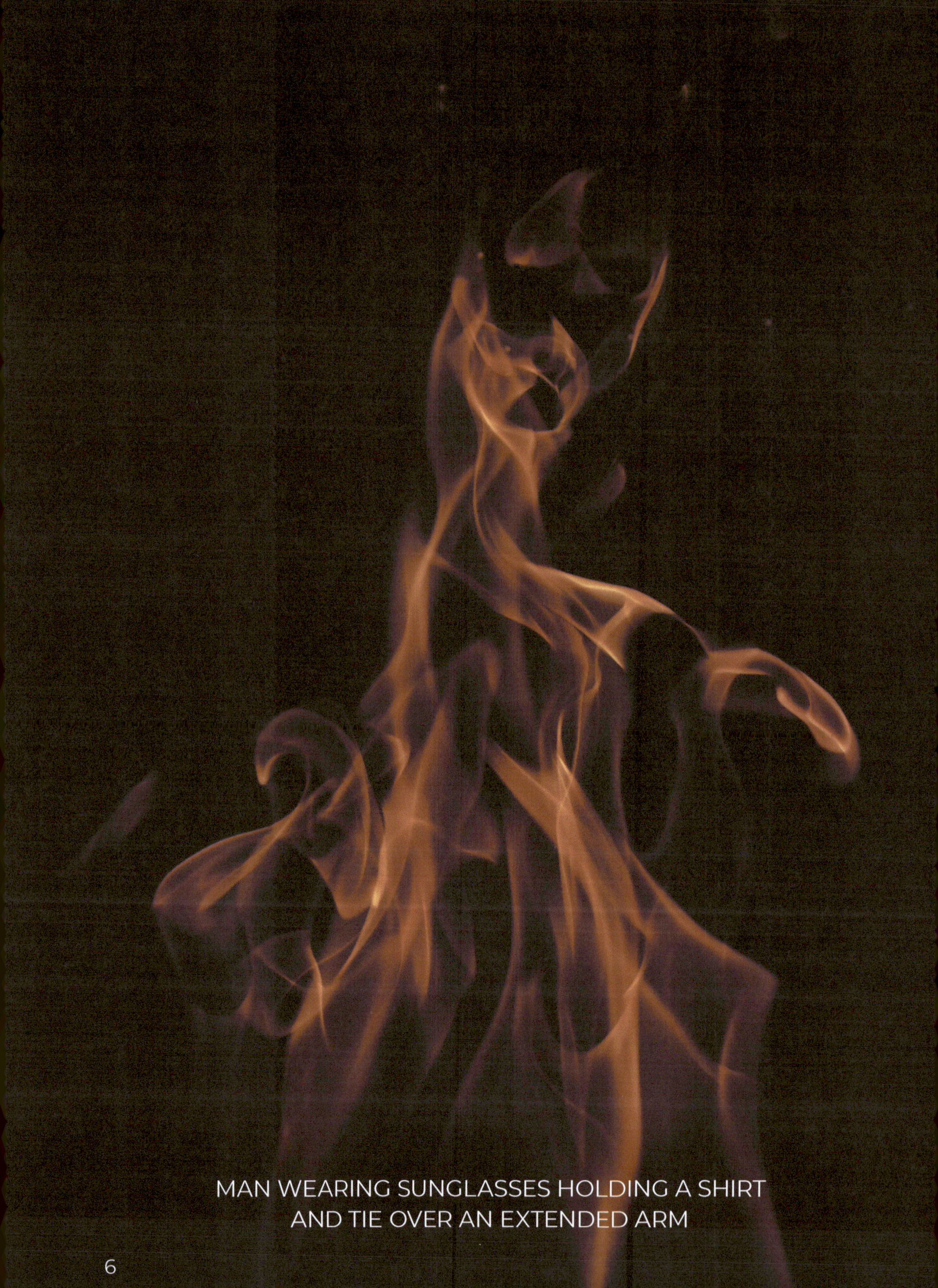

MAN WEARING SUNGLASSES HOLDING A SHIRT
AND TIE OVER AN EXTENDED ARM

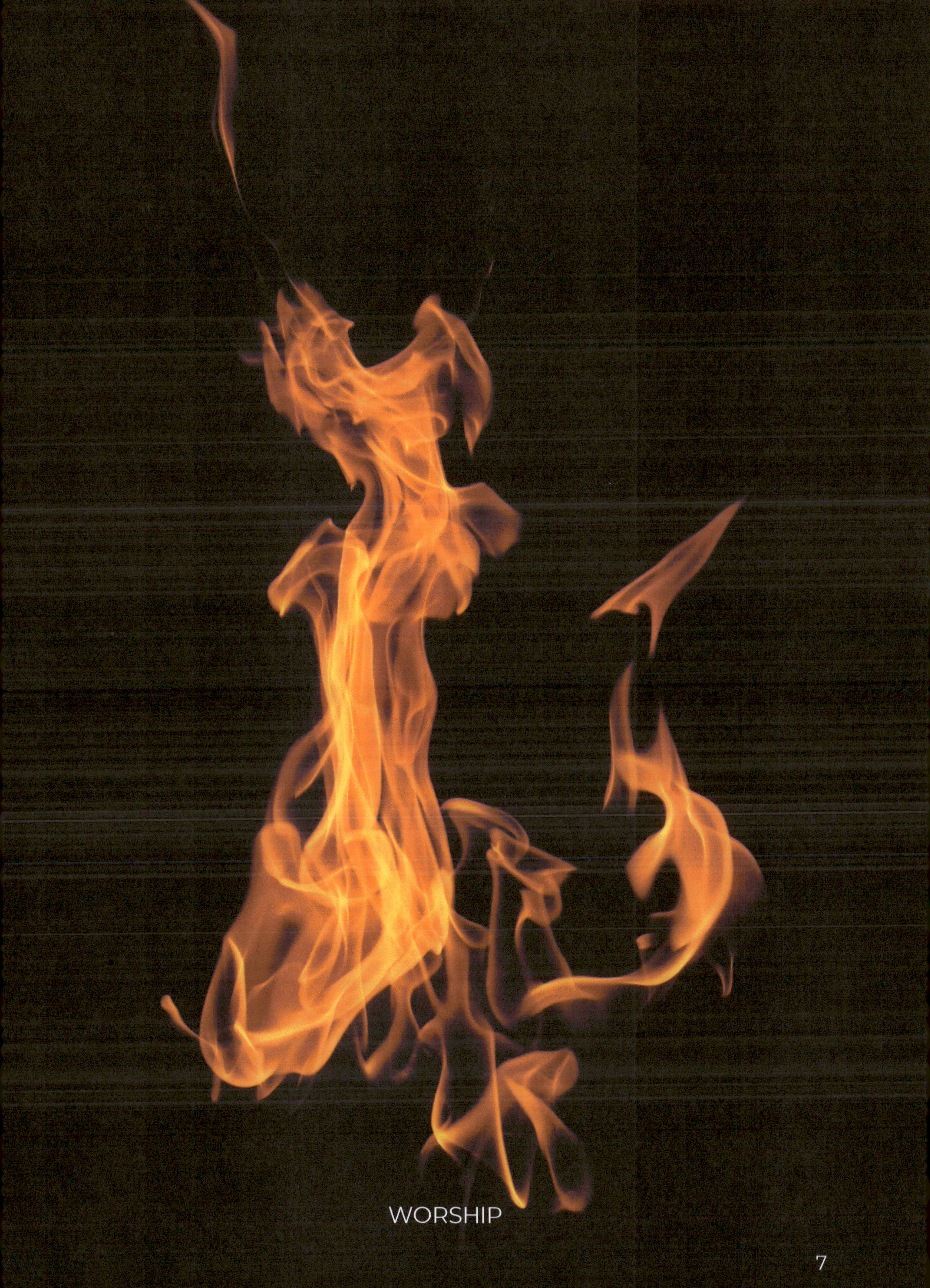

WORSHIP

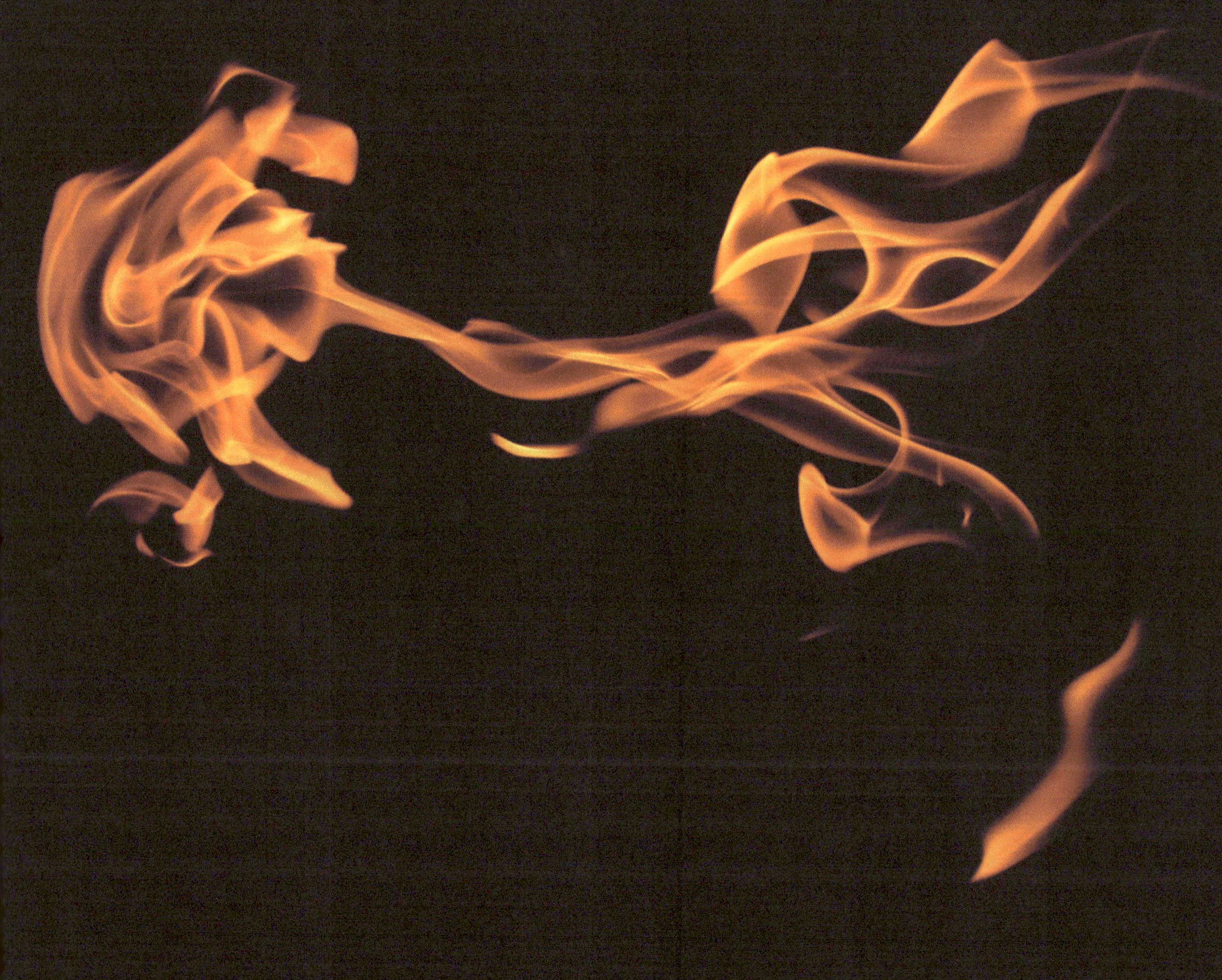

WE MEET THE DRAGON

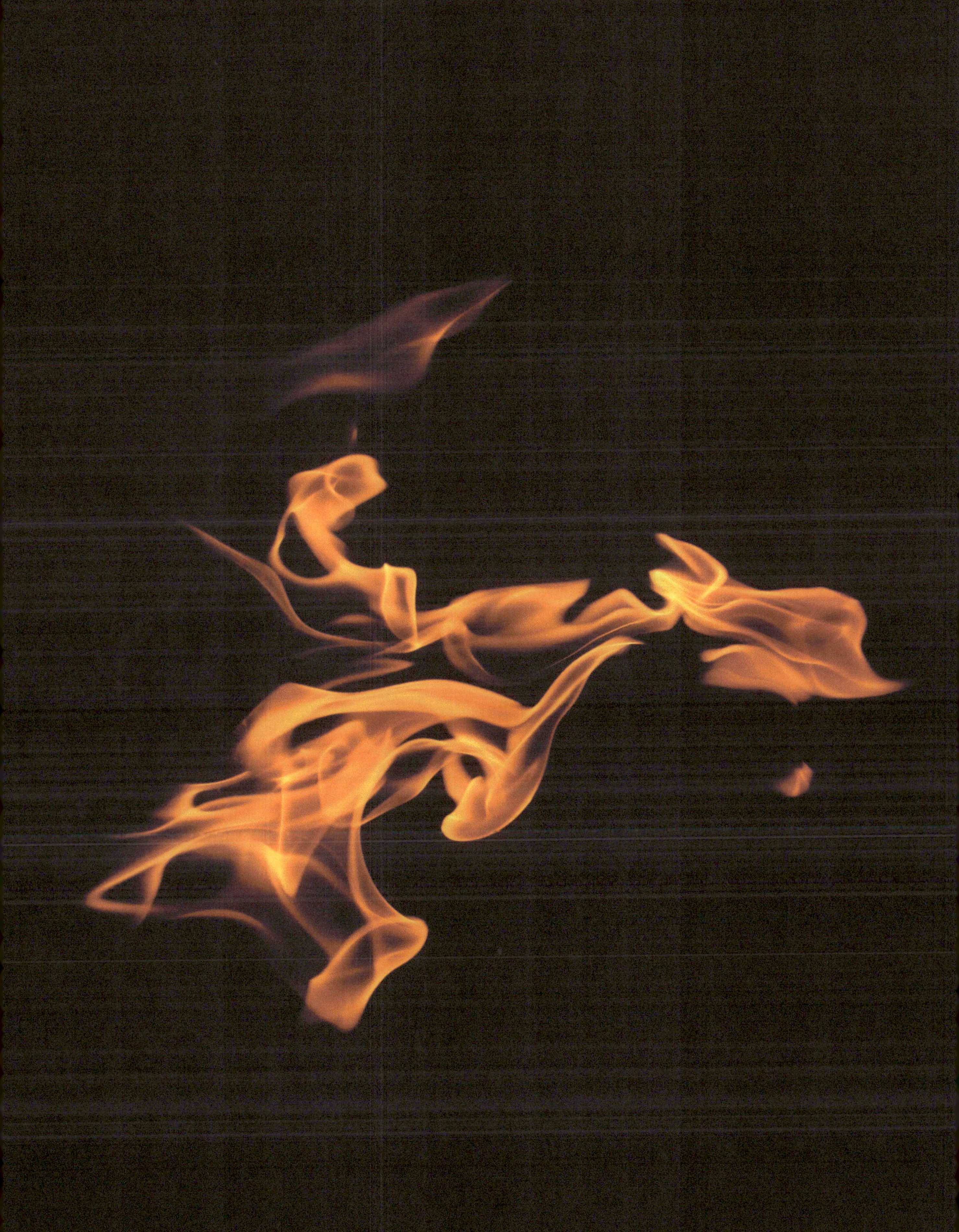

SEATED ON MY DRAGON

THE LOVERS

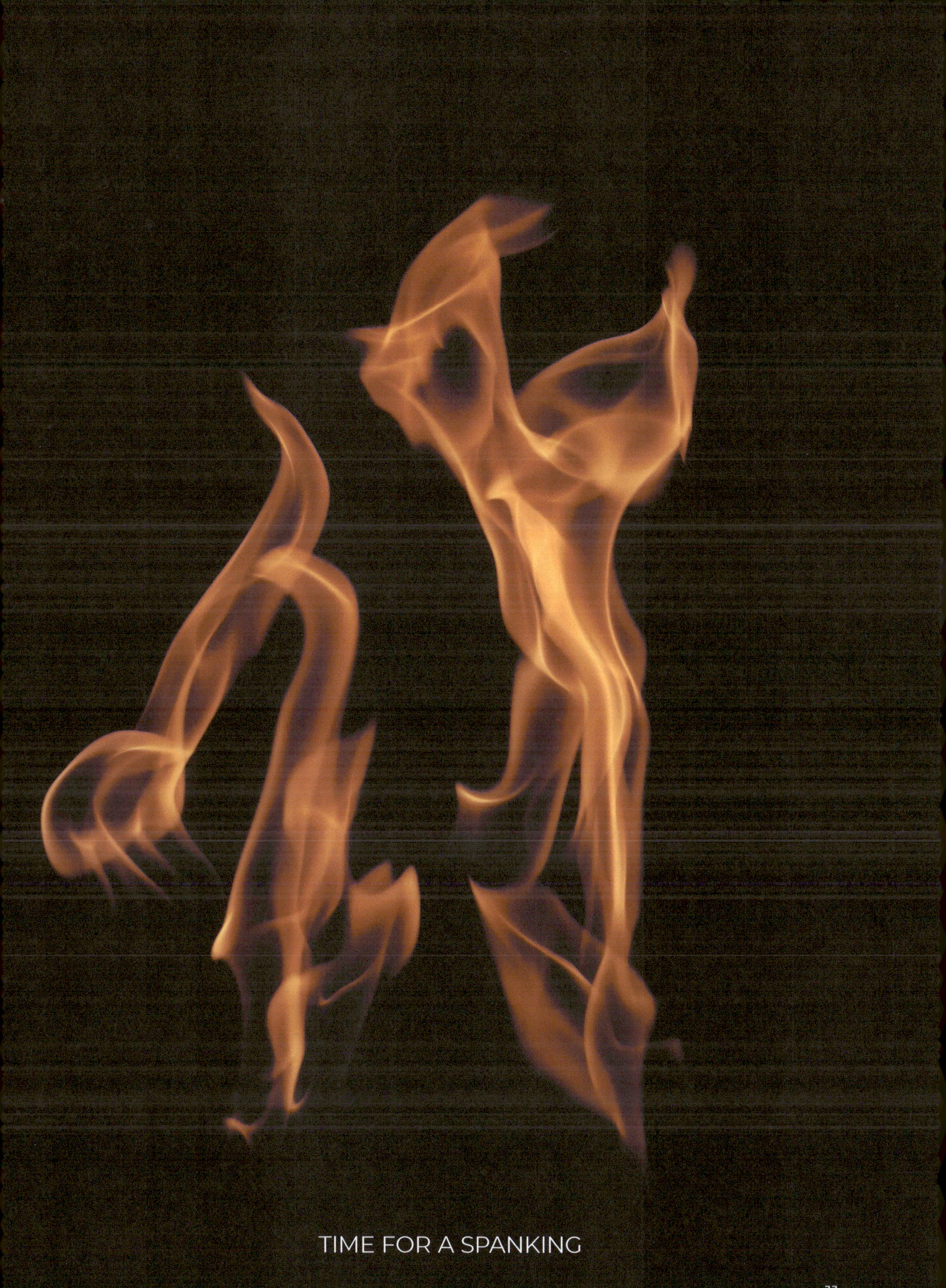

TIME FOR A SPANKING

FLY BABY FLY

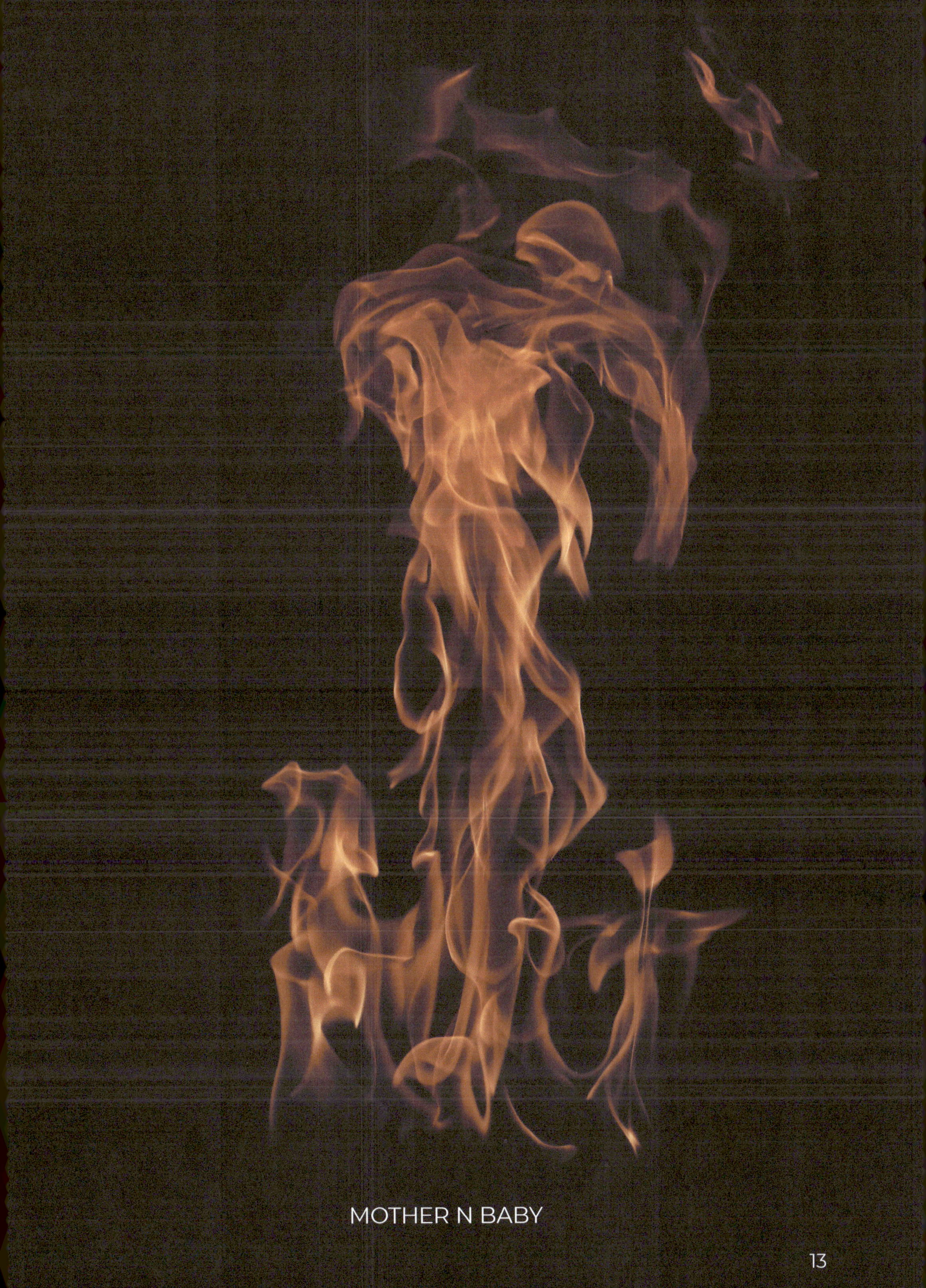

MOTHER N BABY

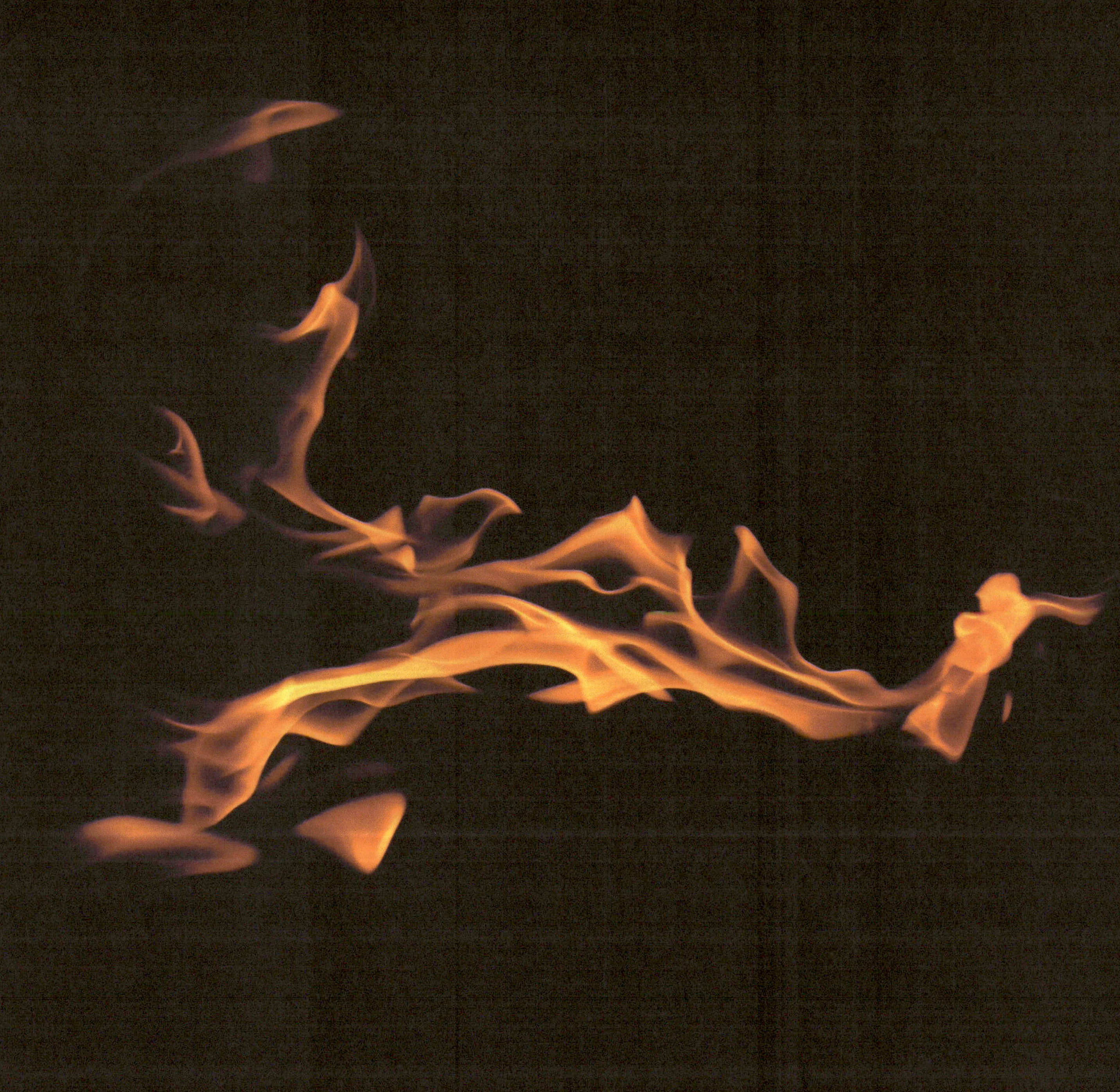

IN THE GRIP OF THE DRAGON

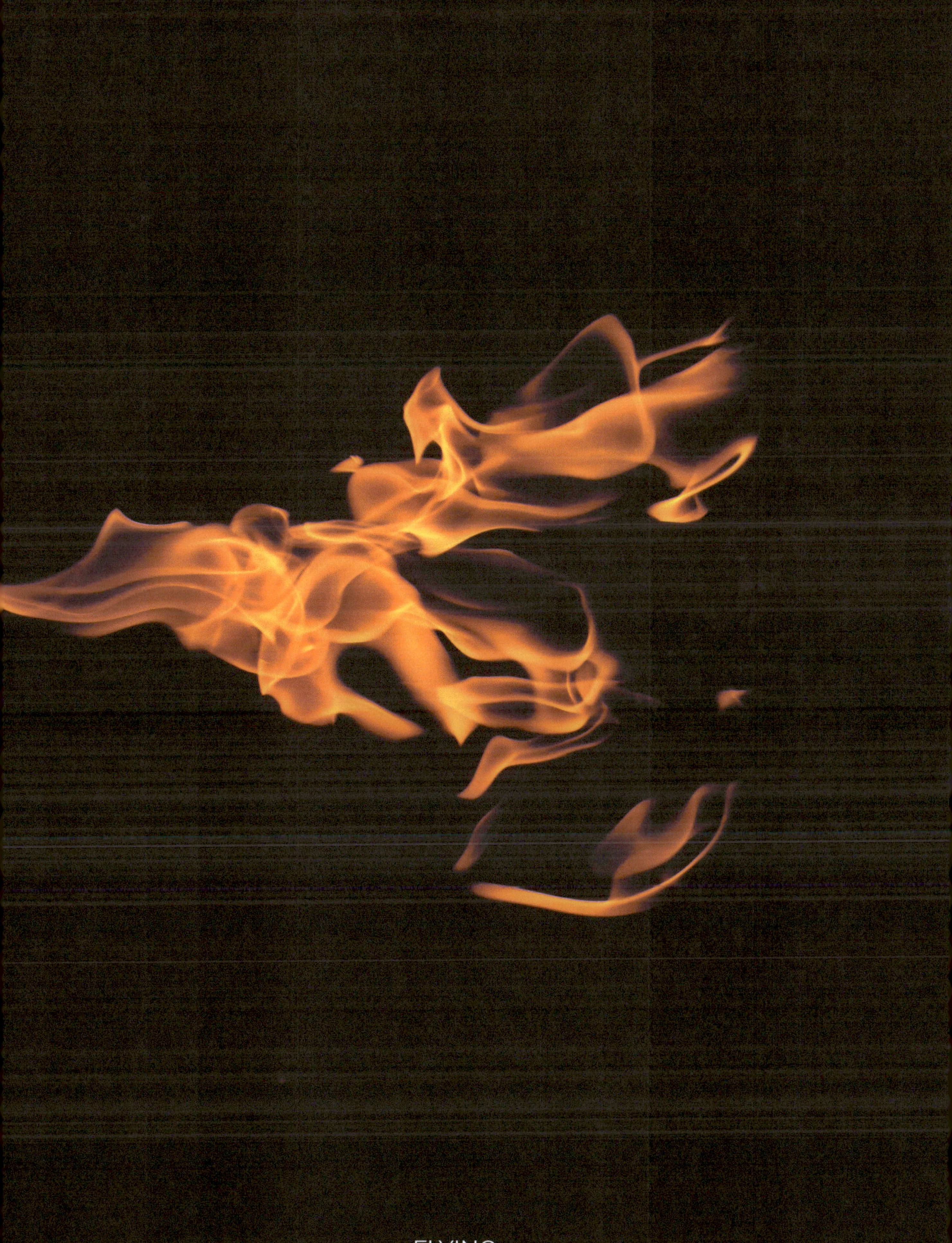

FLYING

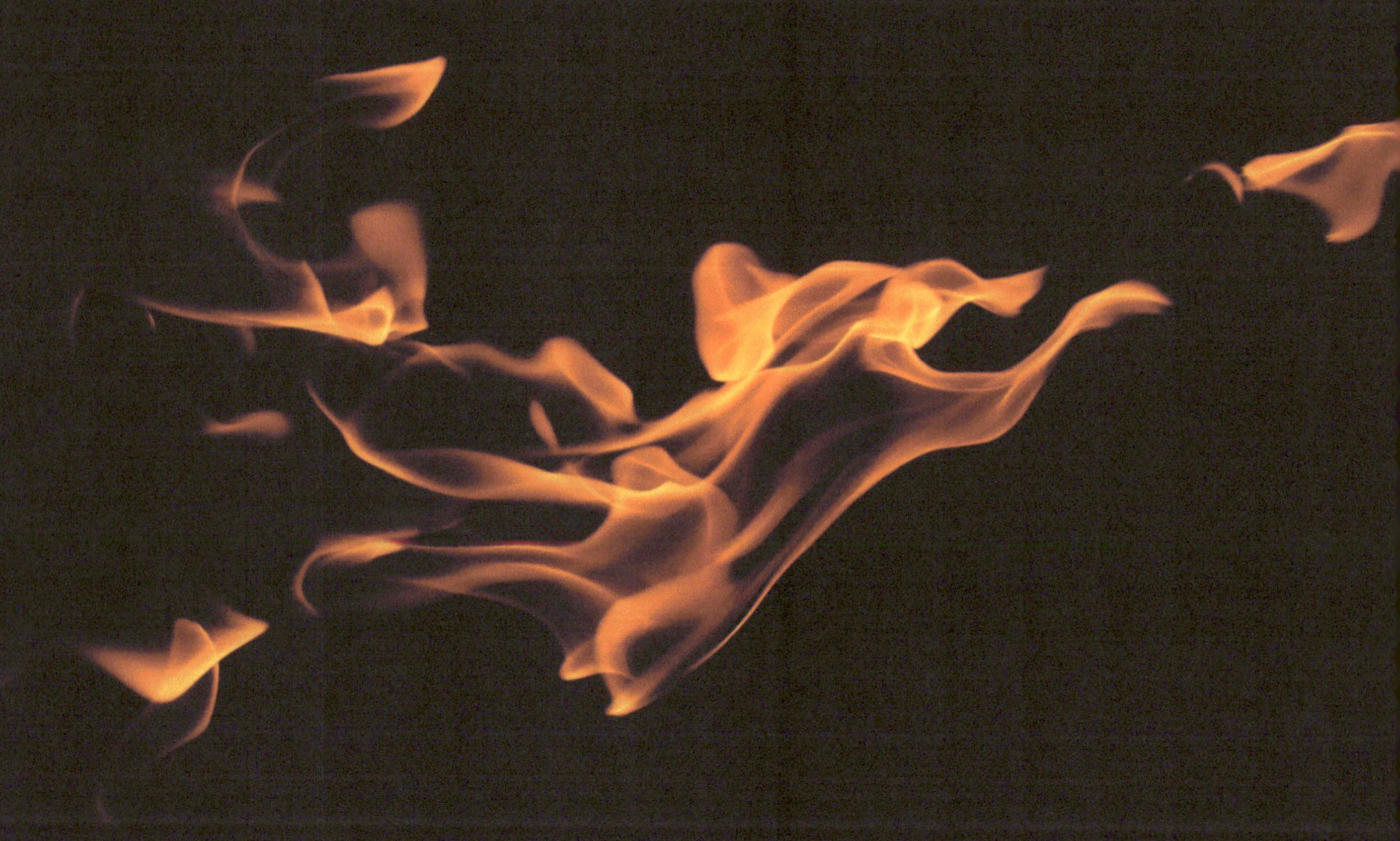

REACHING OUT

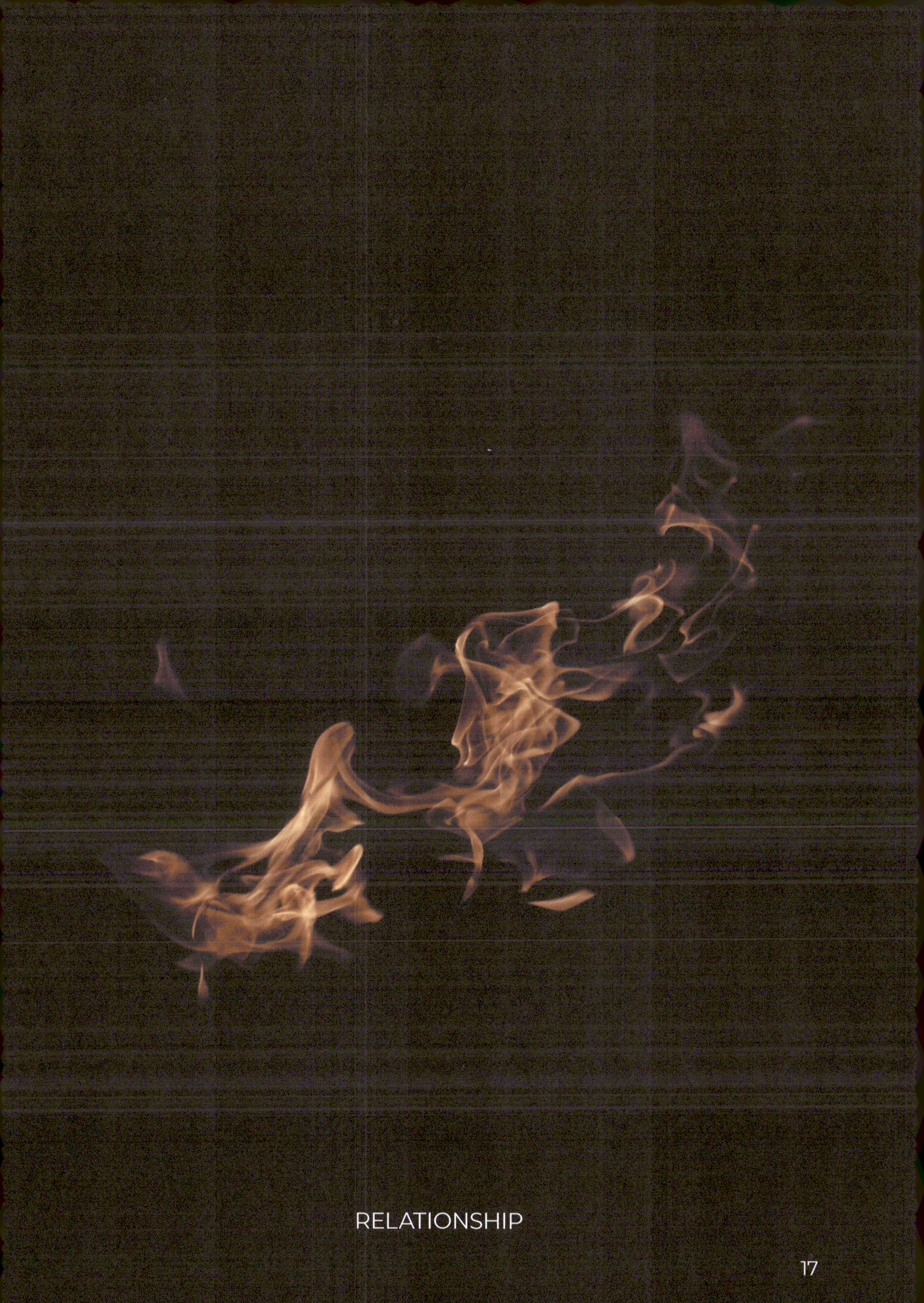

RELATIONSHIP

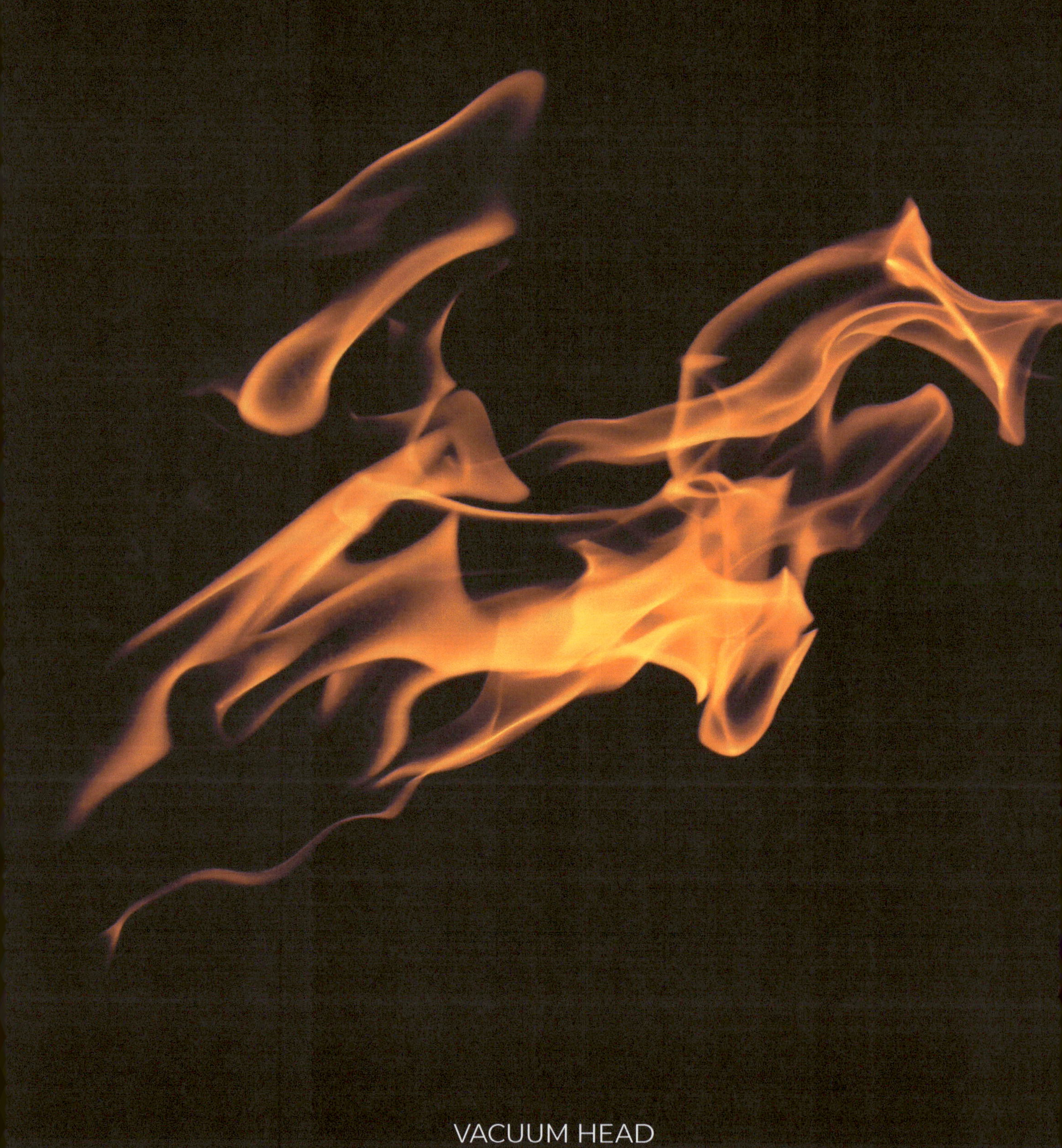

VACUUM HEAD

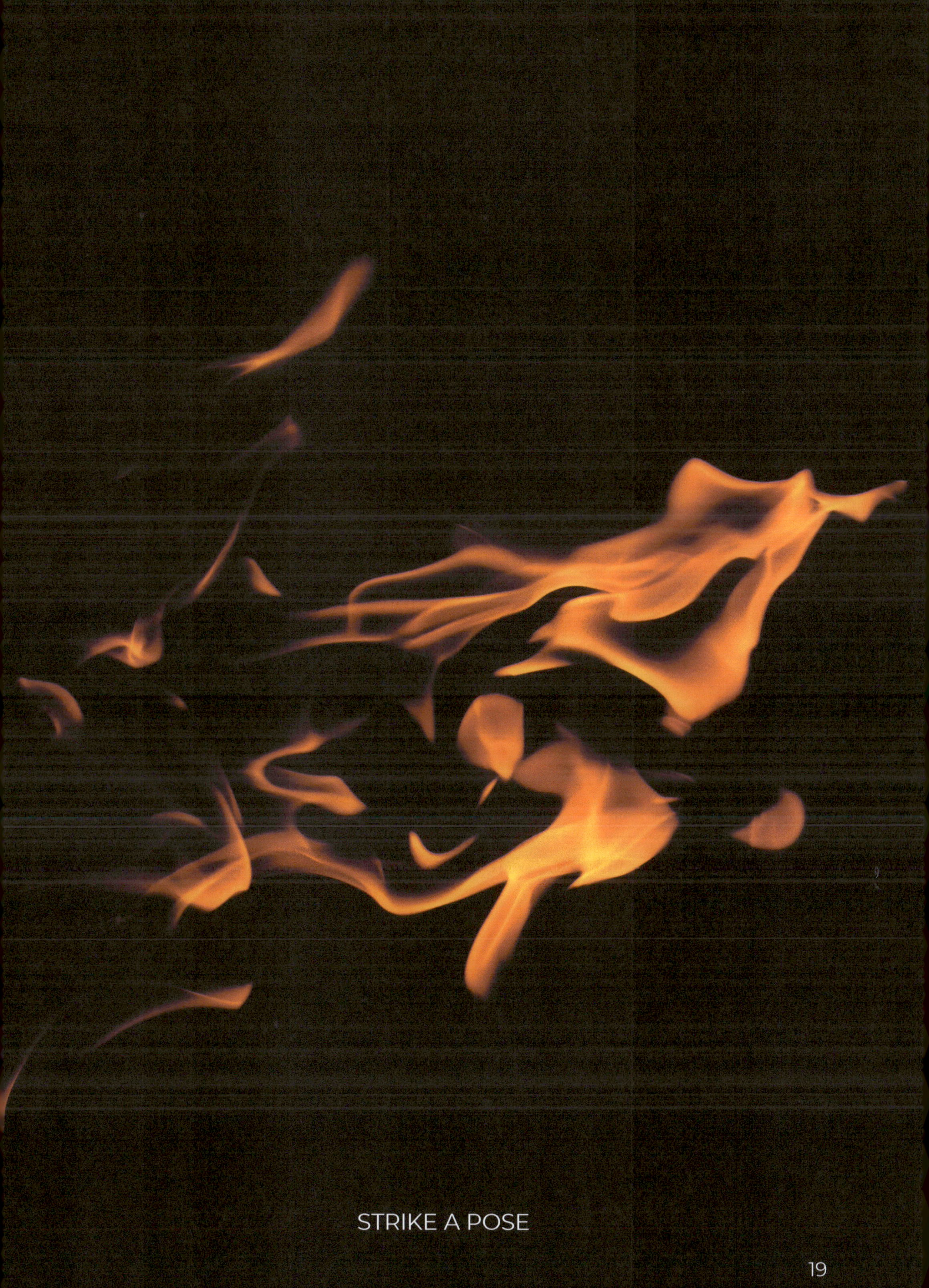

STRIKE A POSE

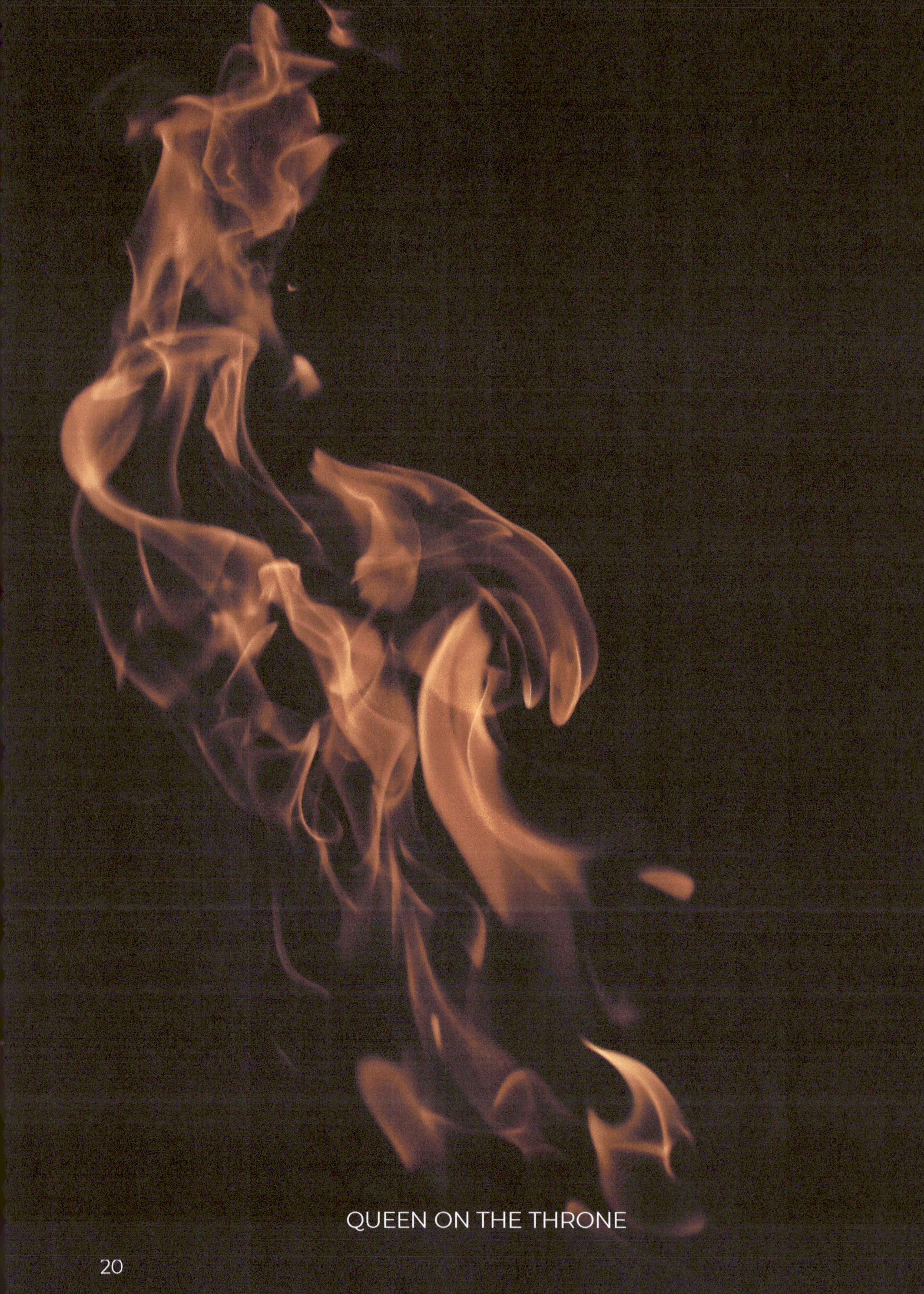

QUEEN ON THE THRONE

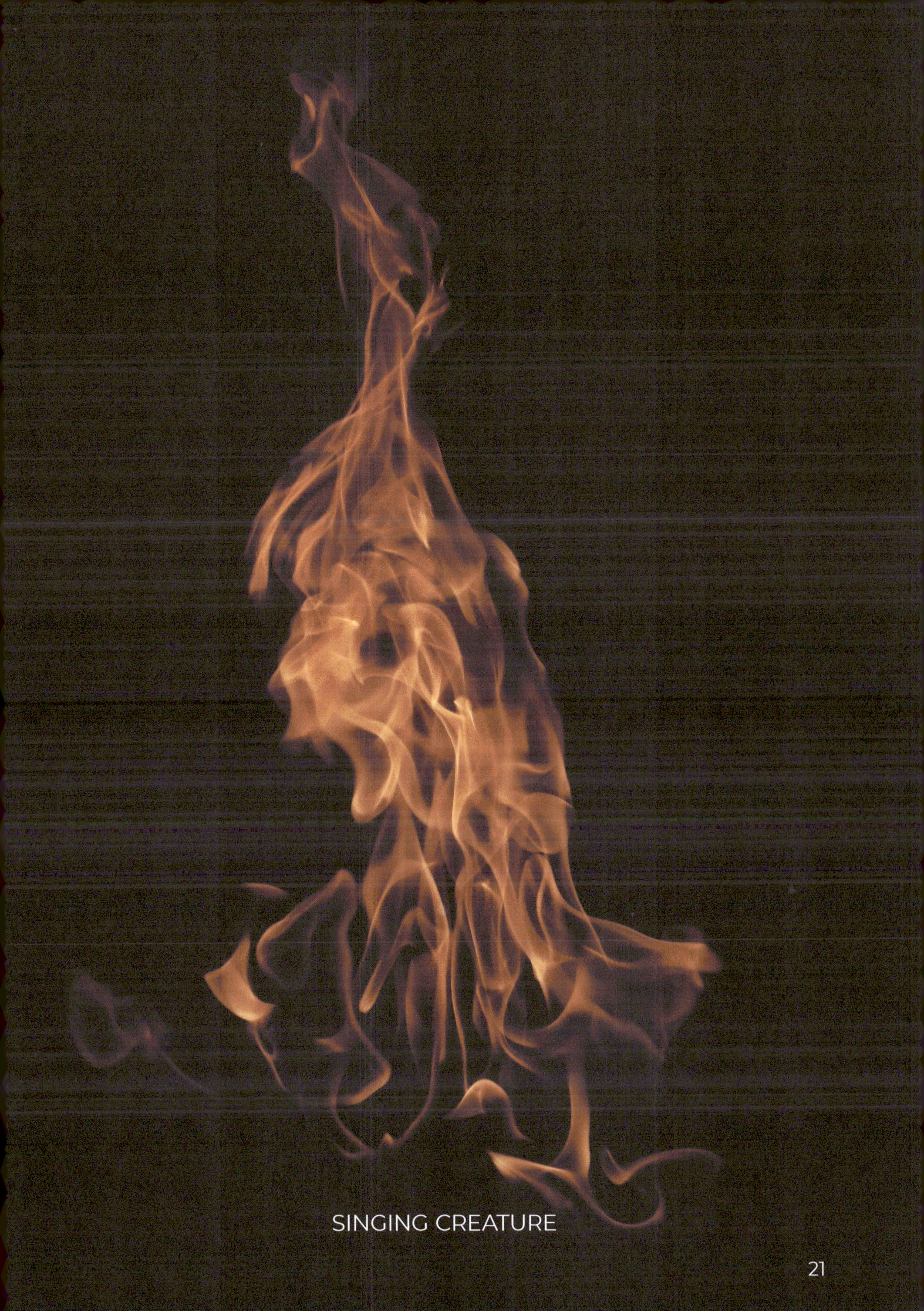

SINGING CREATURE

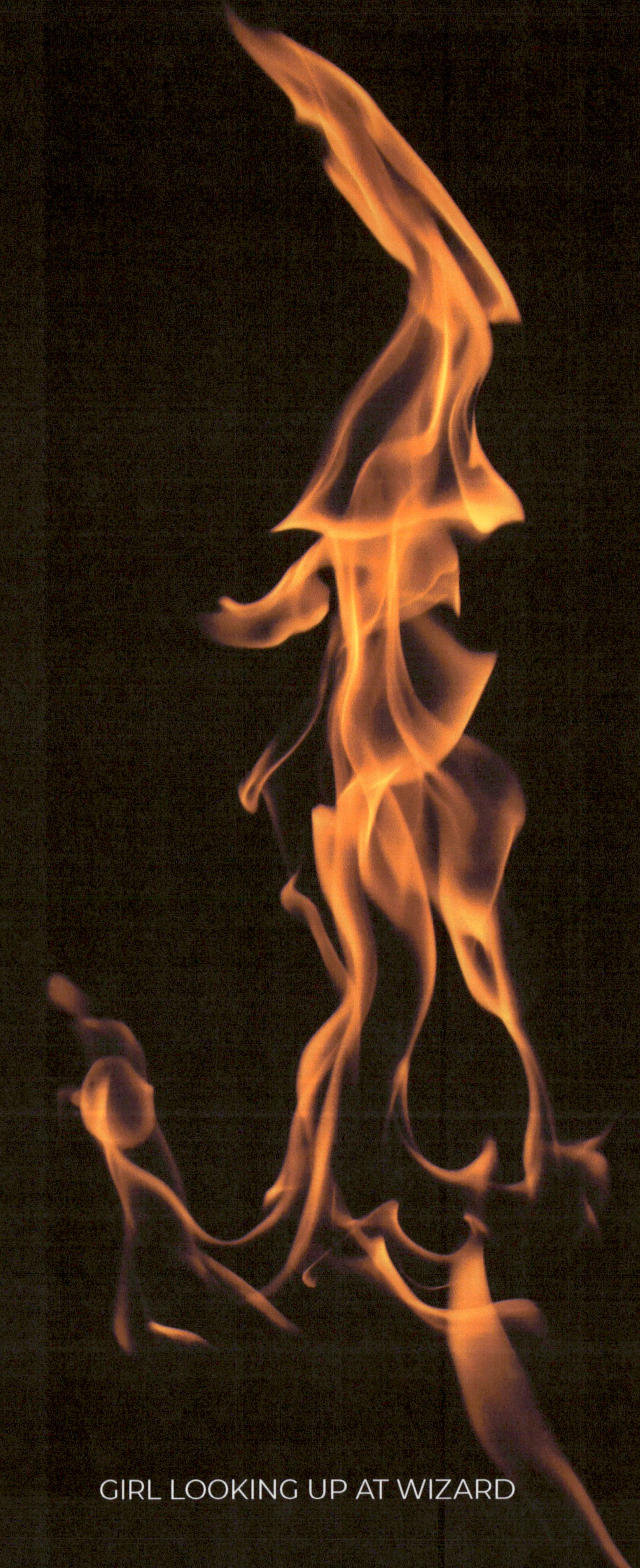

GIRL LOOKING UP AT WIZARD

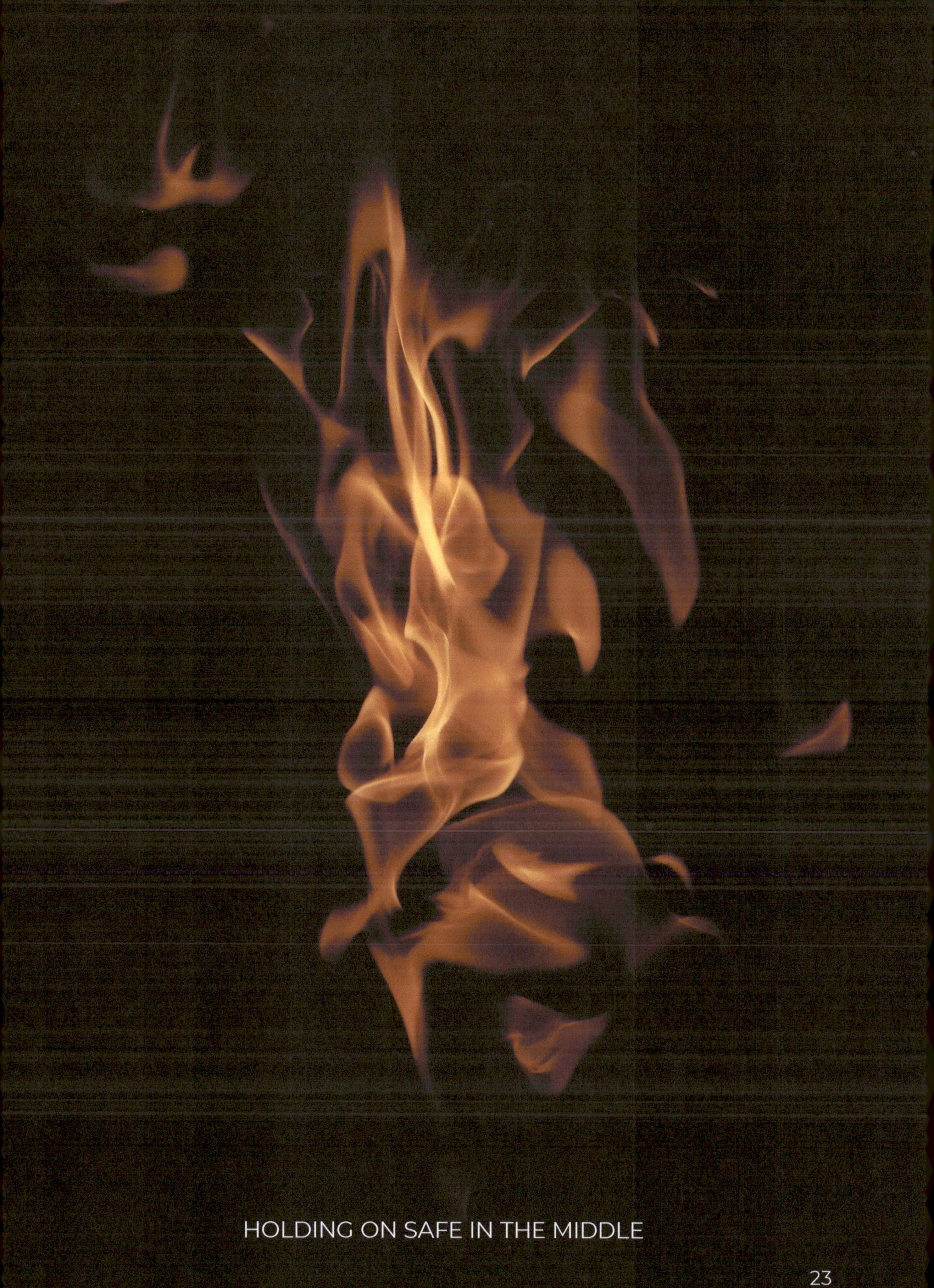

HOLDING ON SAFE IN THE MIDDLE

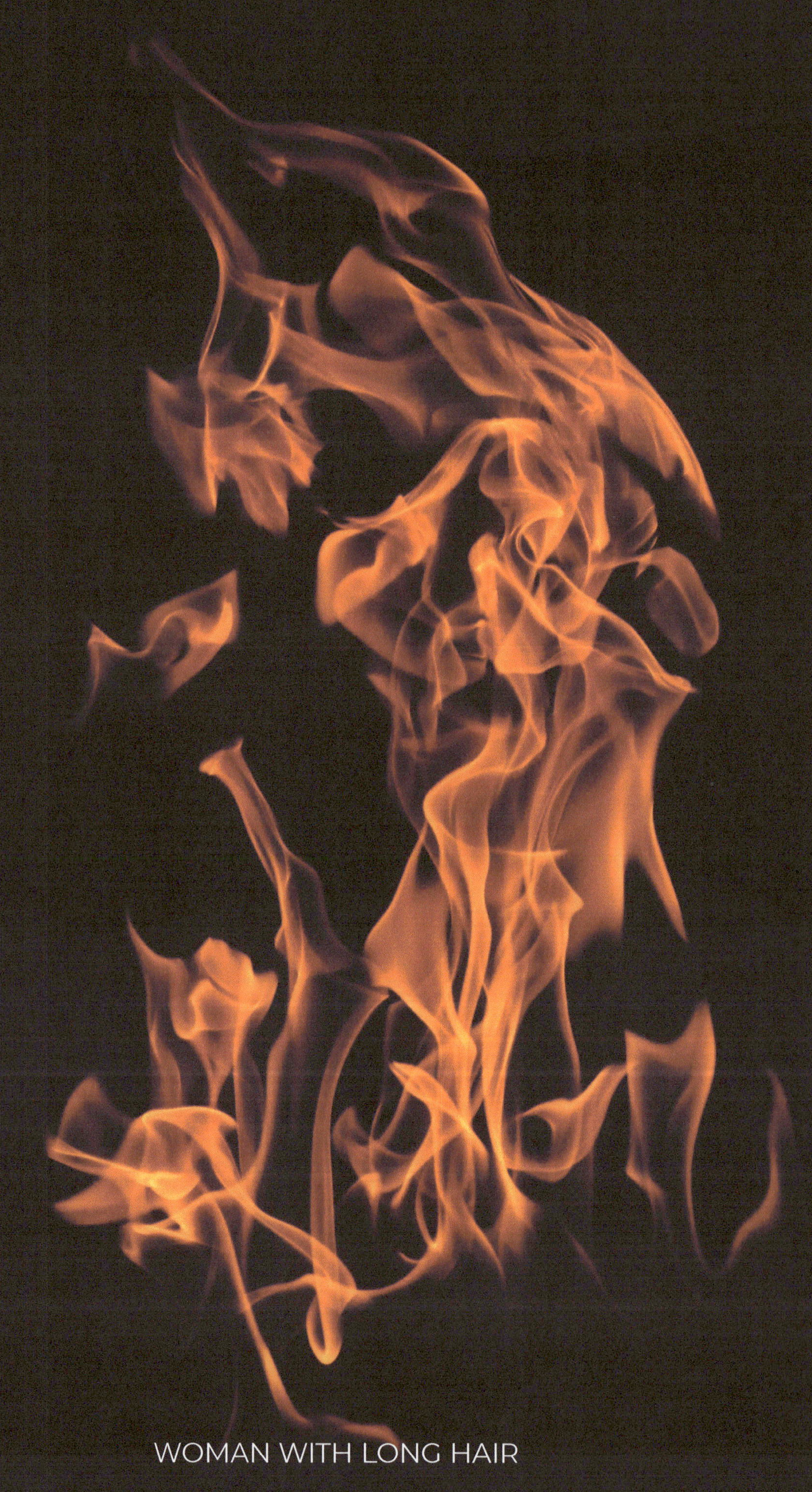

WOMAN WITH LONG HAIR

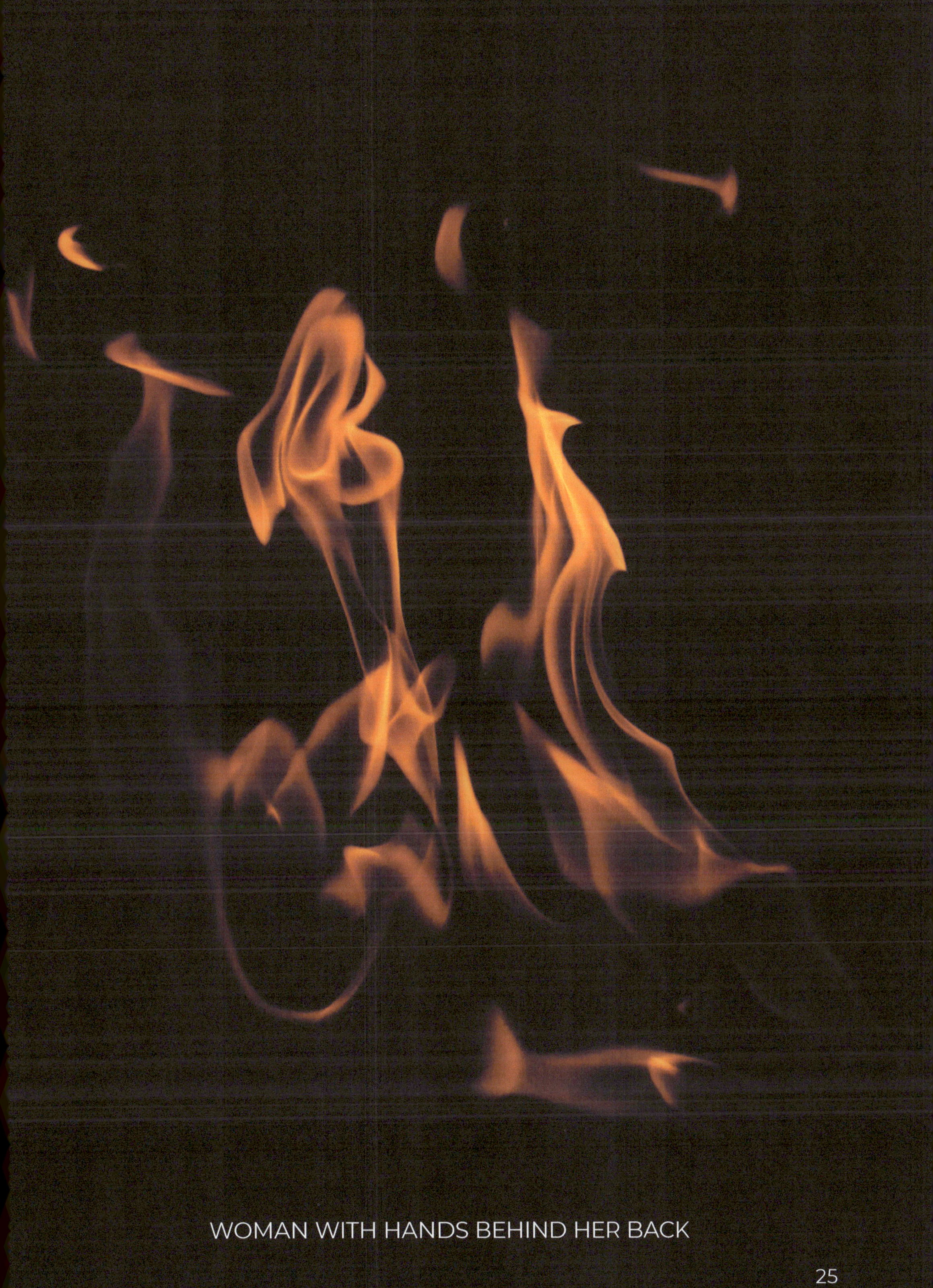

WOMAN WITH HANDS BEHIND HER BACK

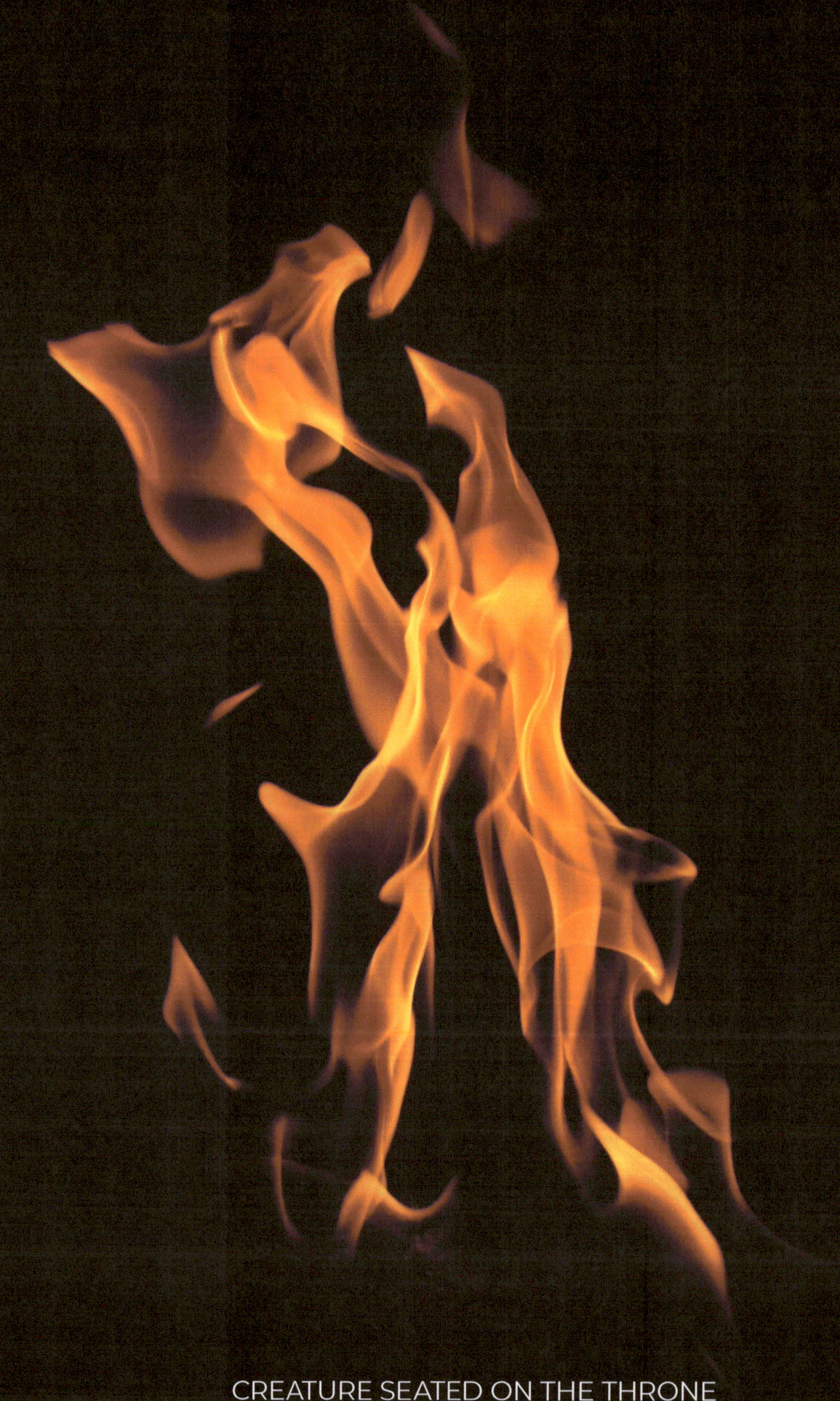

CREATURE SEATED ON THE THRONE

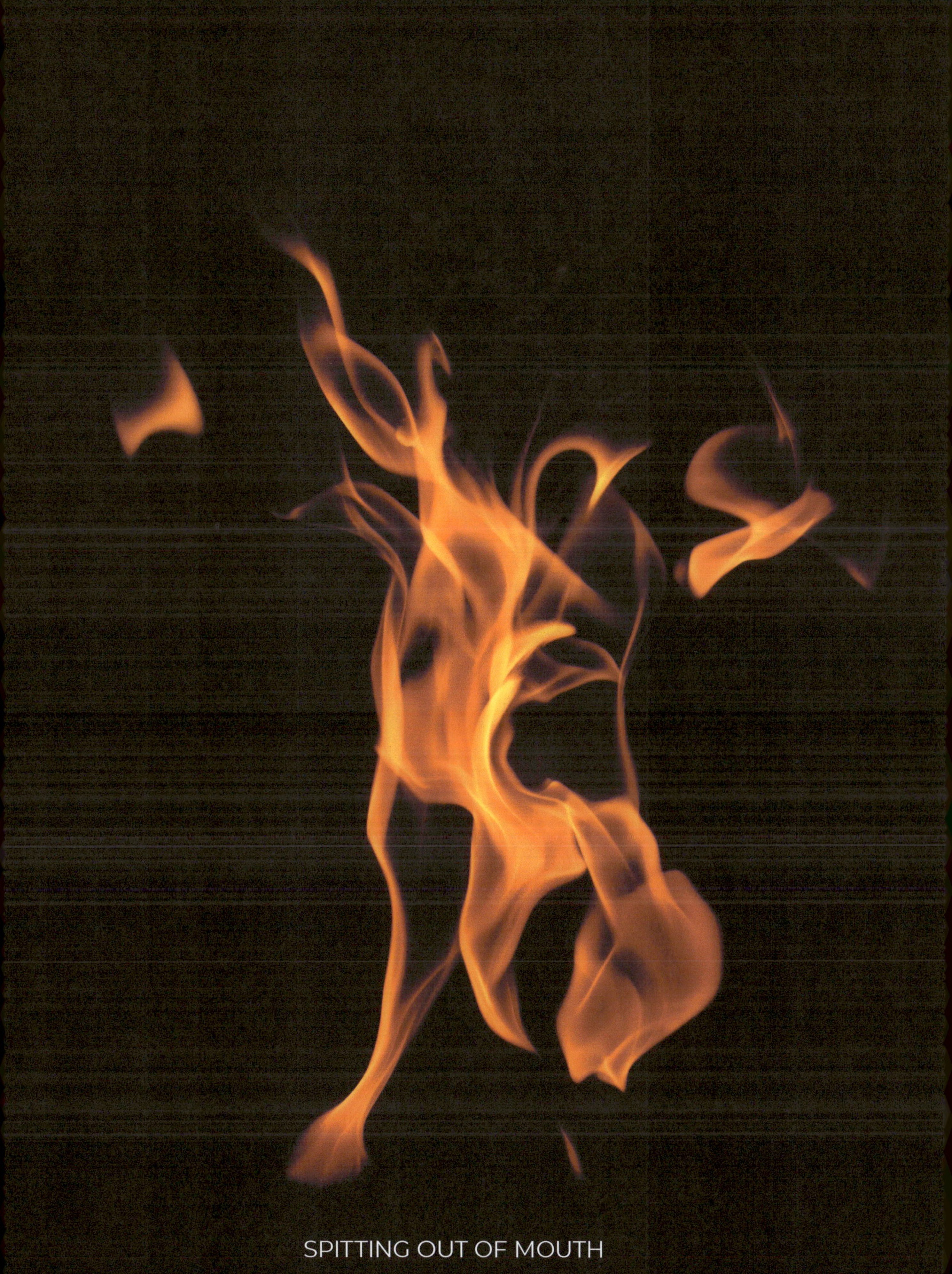

SPITTING OUT OF MOUTH

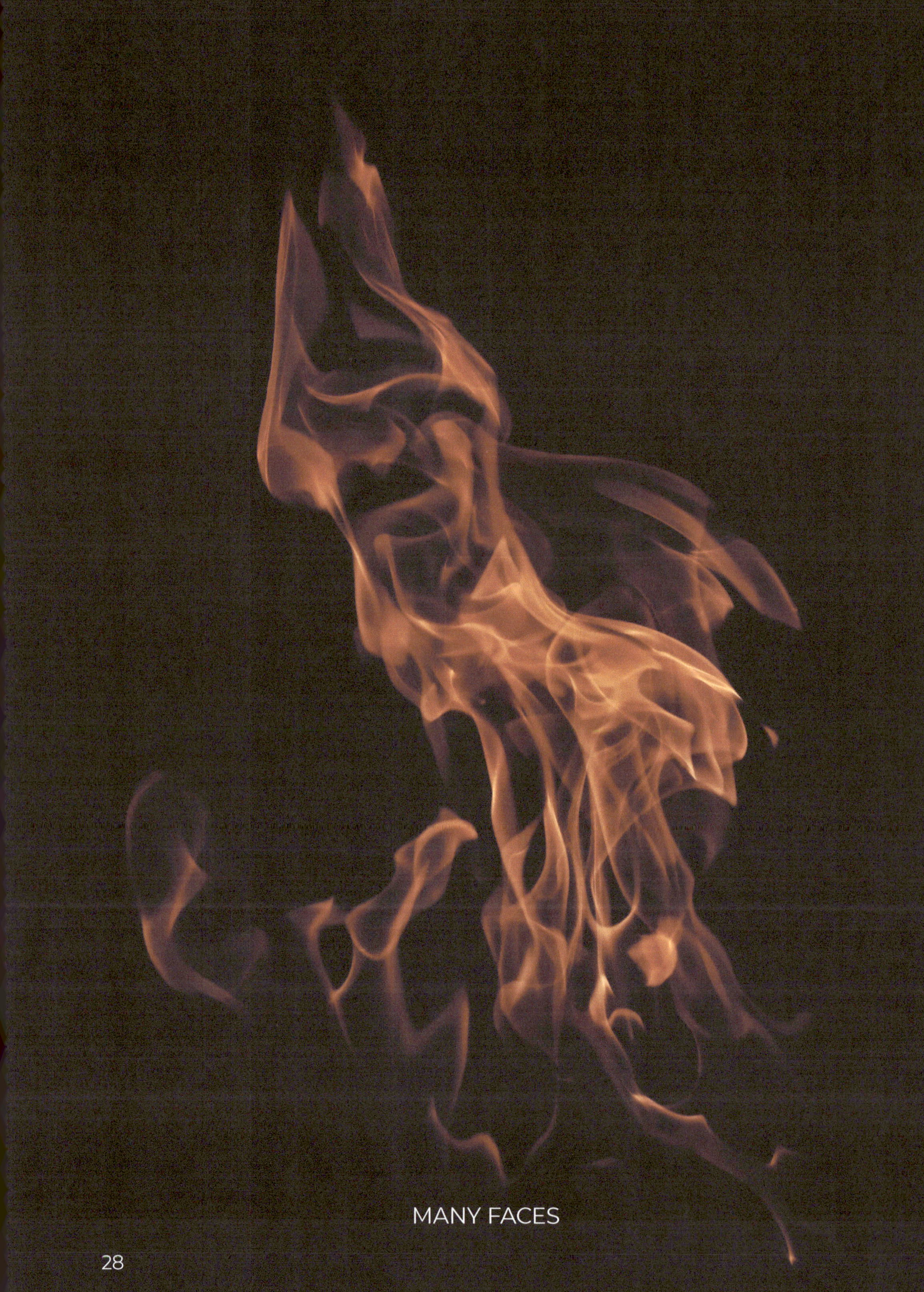

MANY FACES

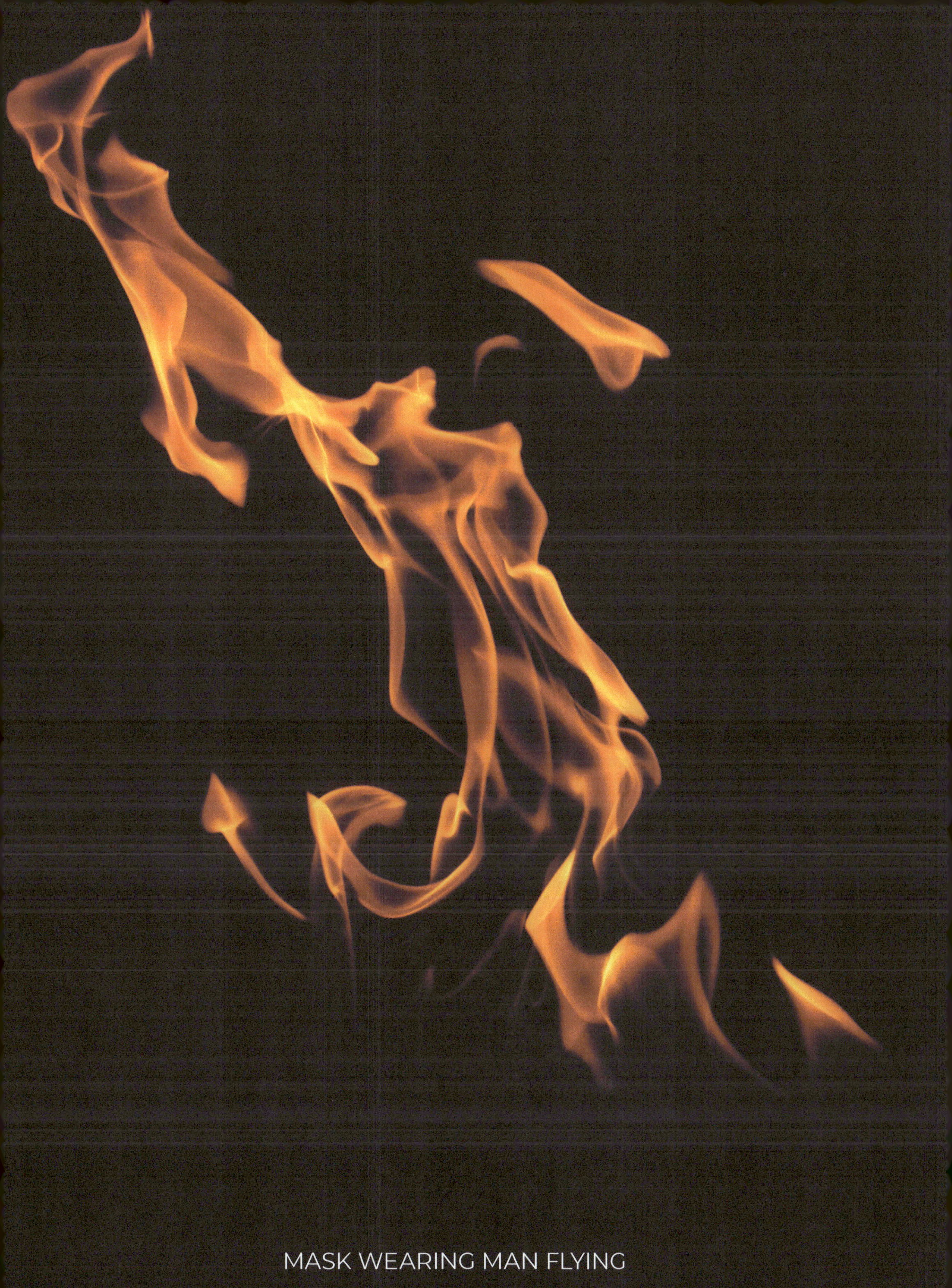

MASK WEARING MAN FLYING

BE SEATED

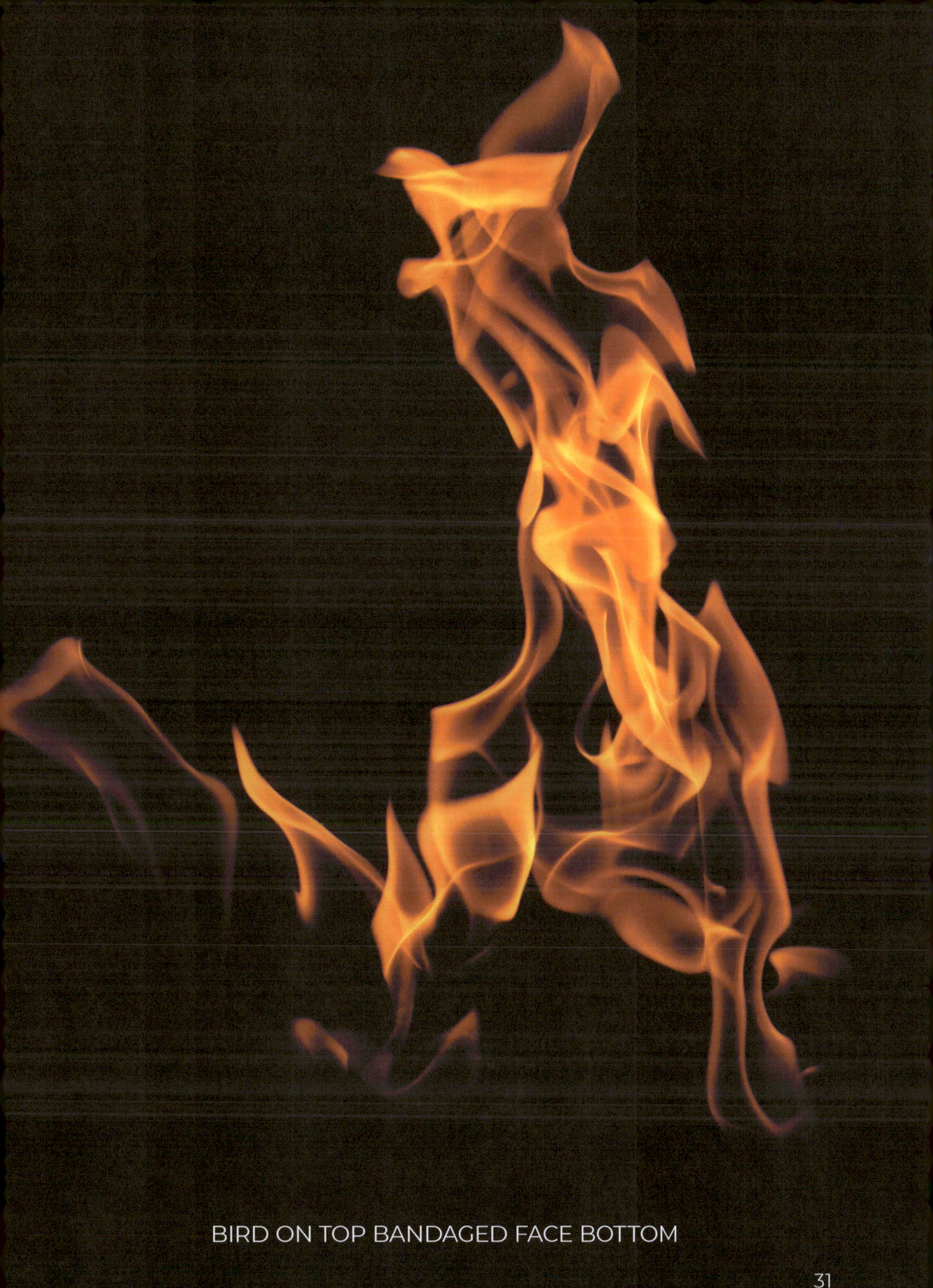

BIRD ON TOP BANDAGED FACE BOTTOM

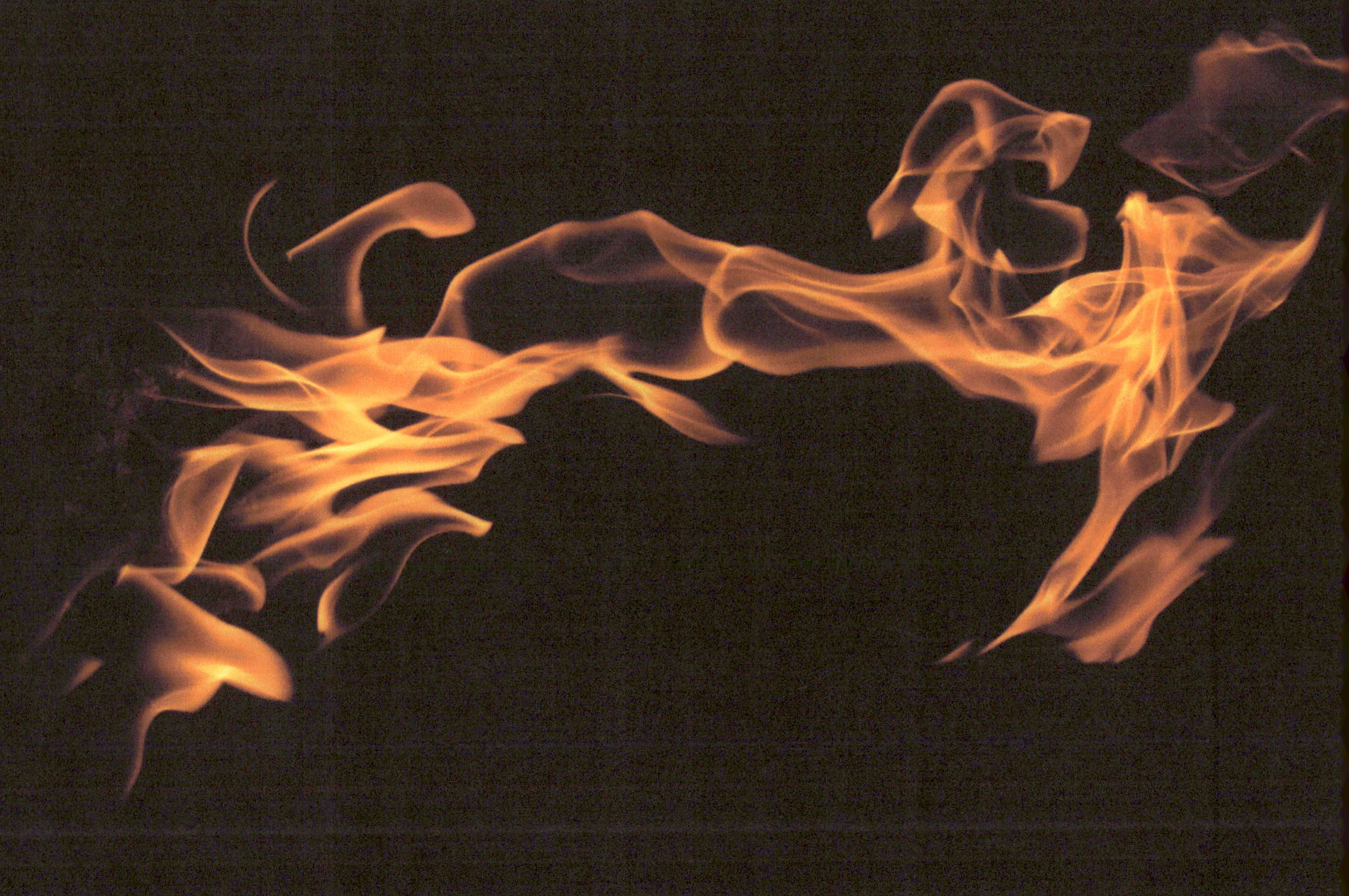

DOG HOLDING A MAN

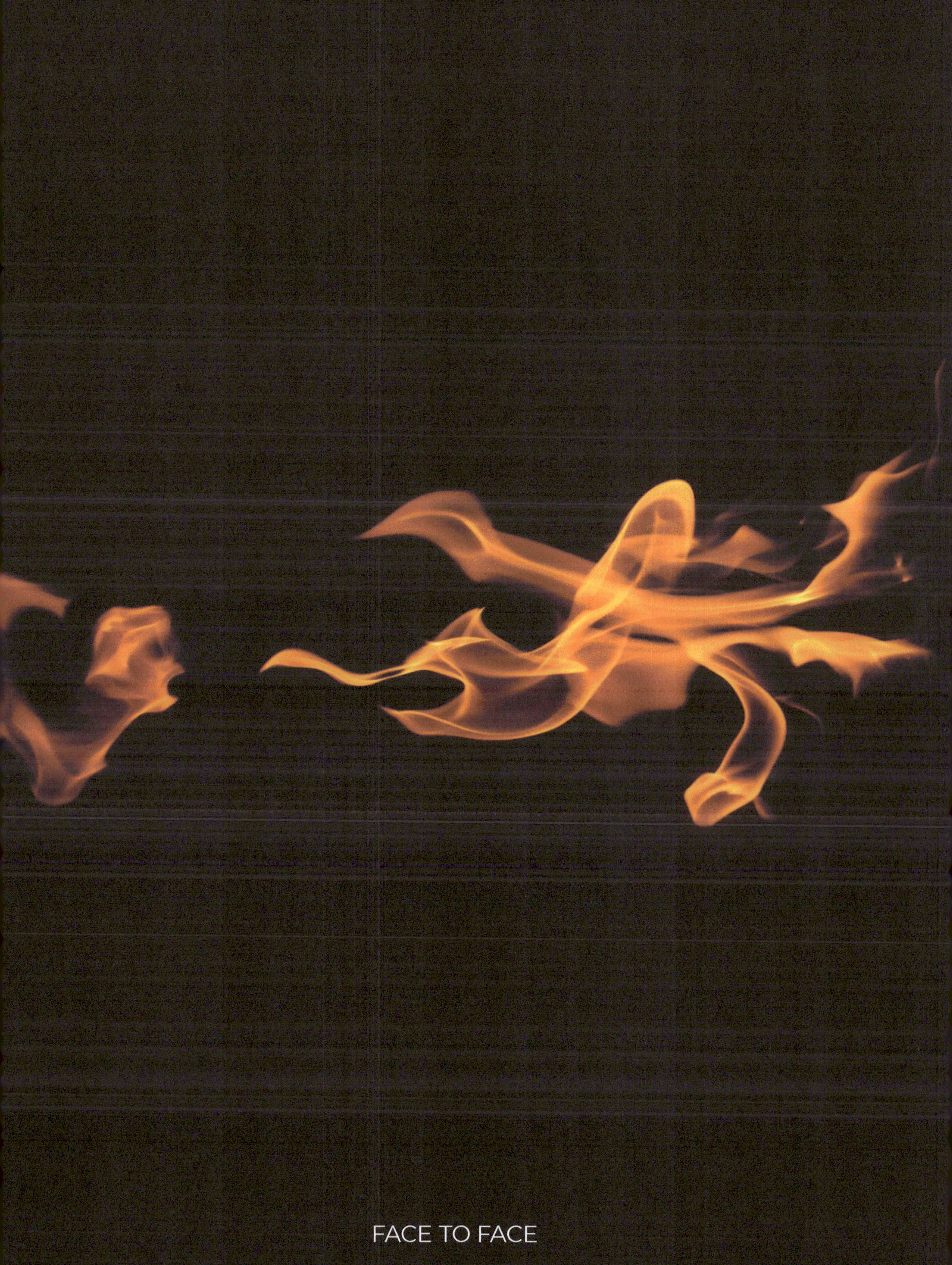

FACE TO FACE

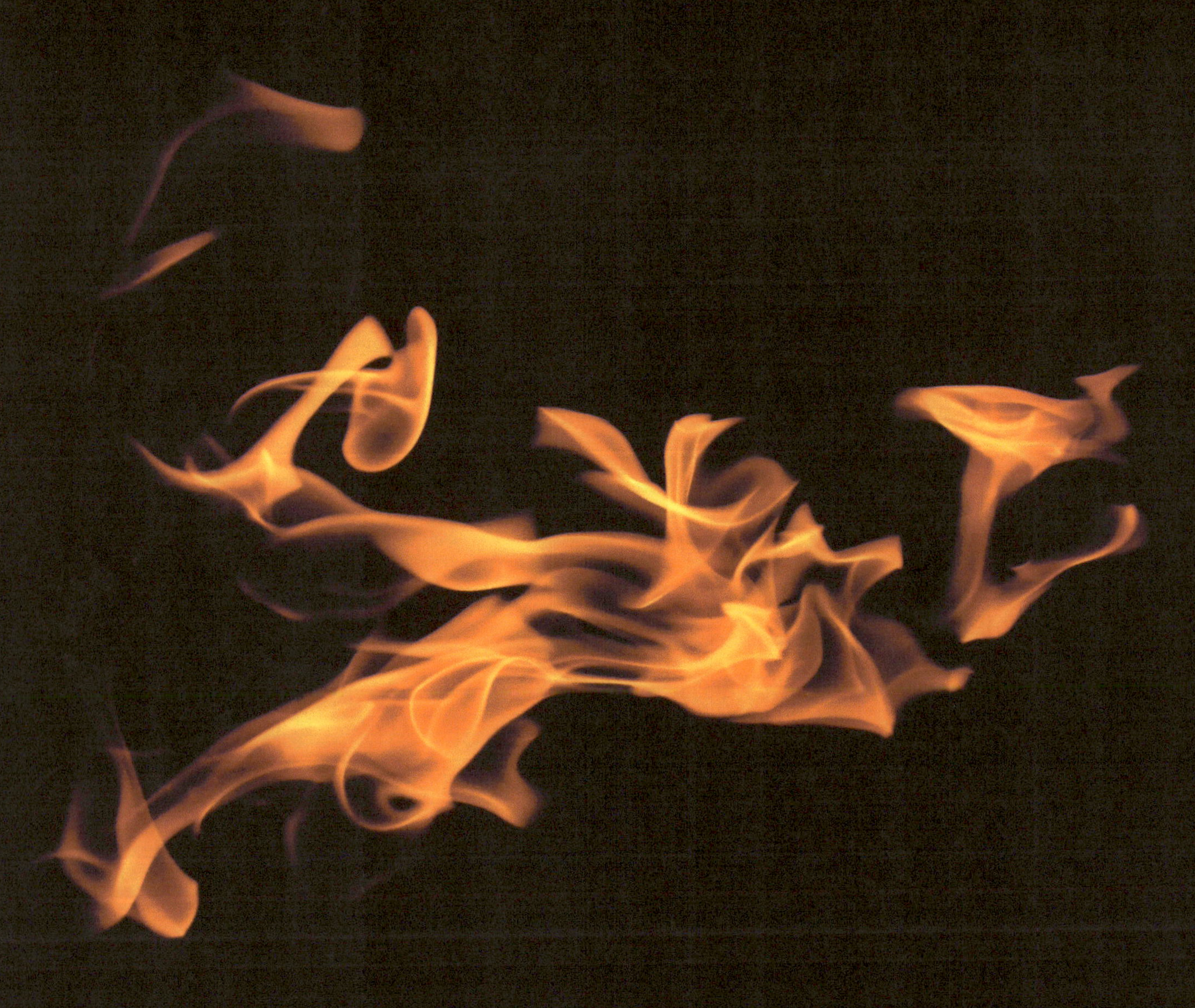

HUNGRY DRAGON X

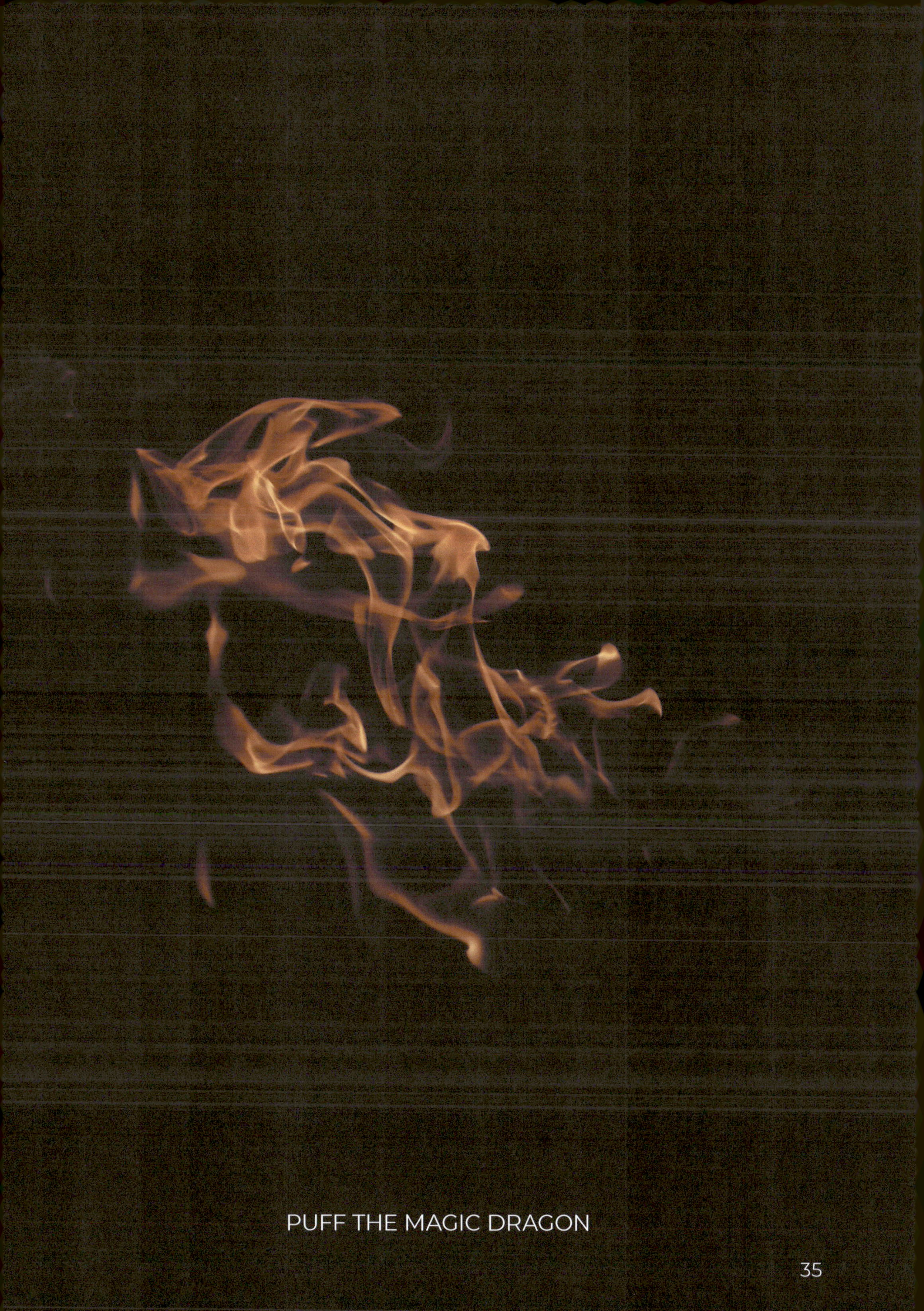

PUFF THE MAGIC DRAGON

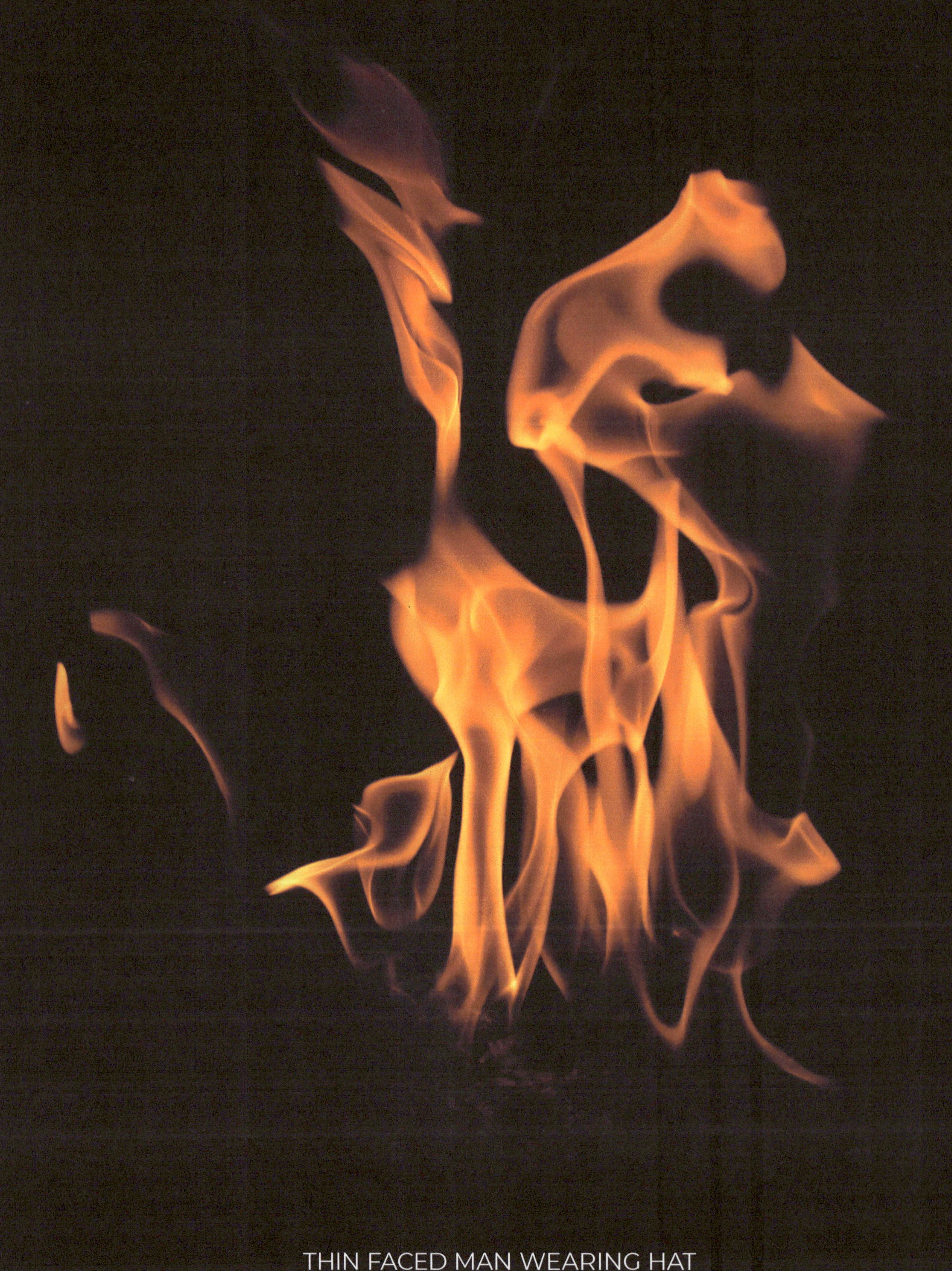

THIN FACED MAN WEARING HAT

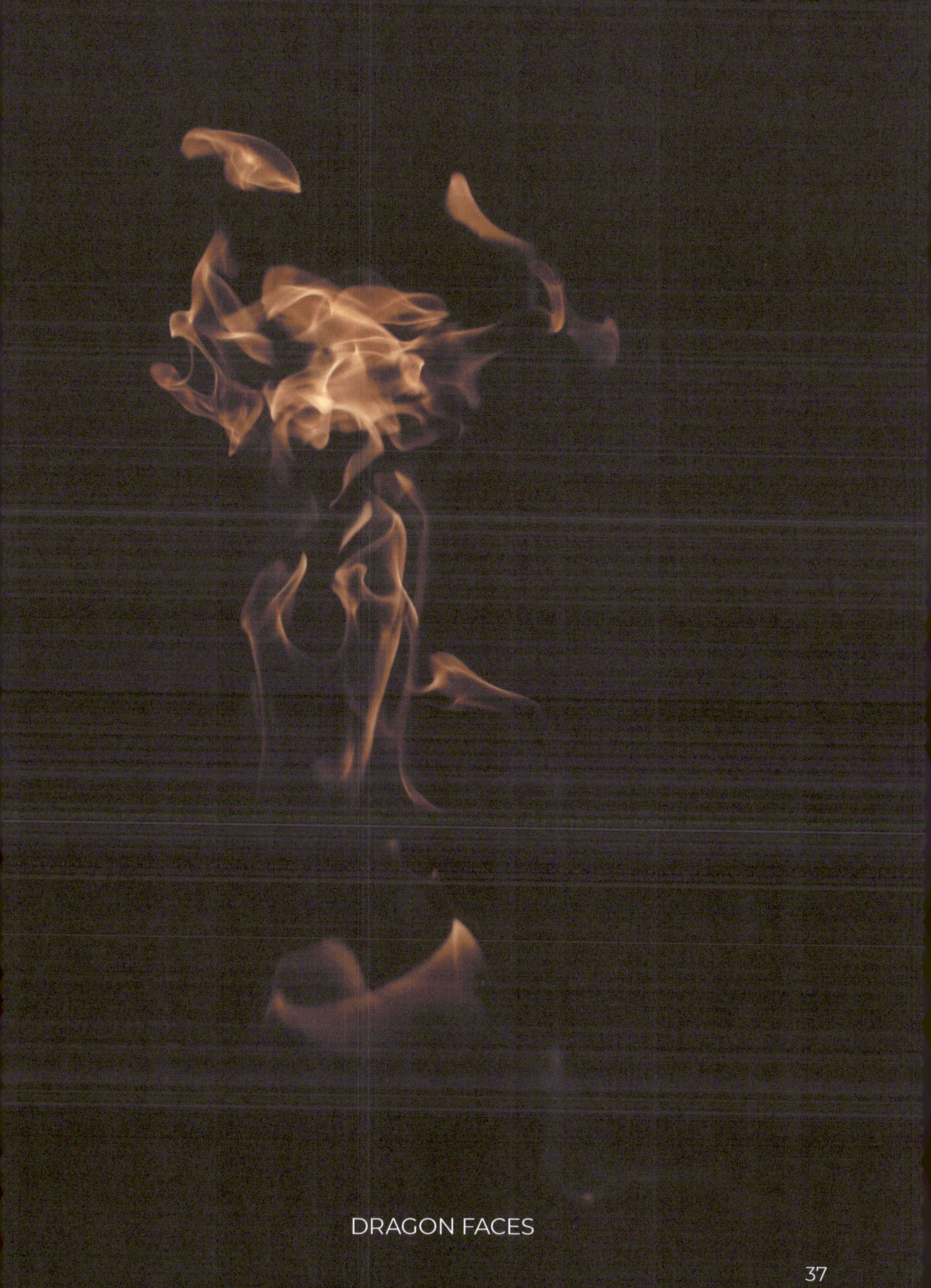

DRAGON FACES

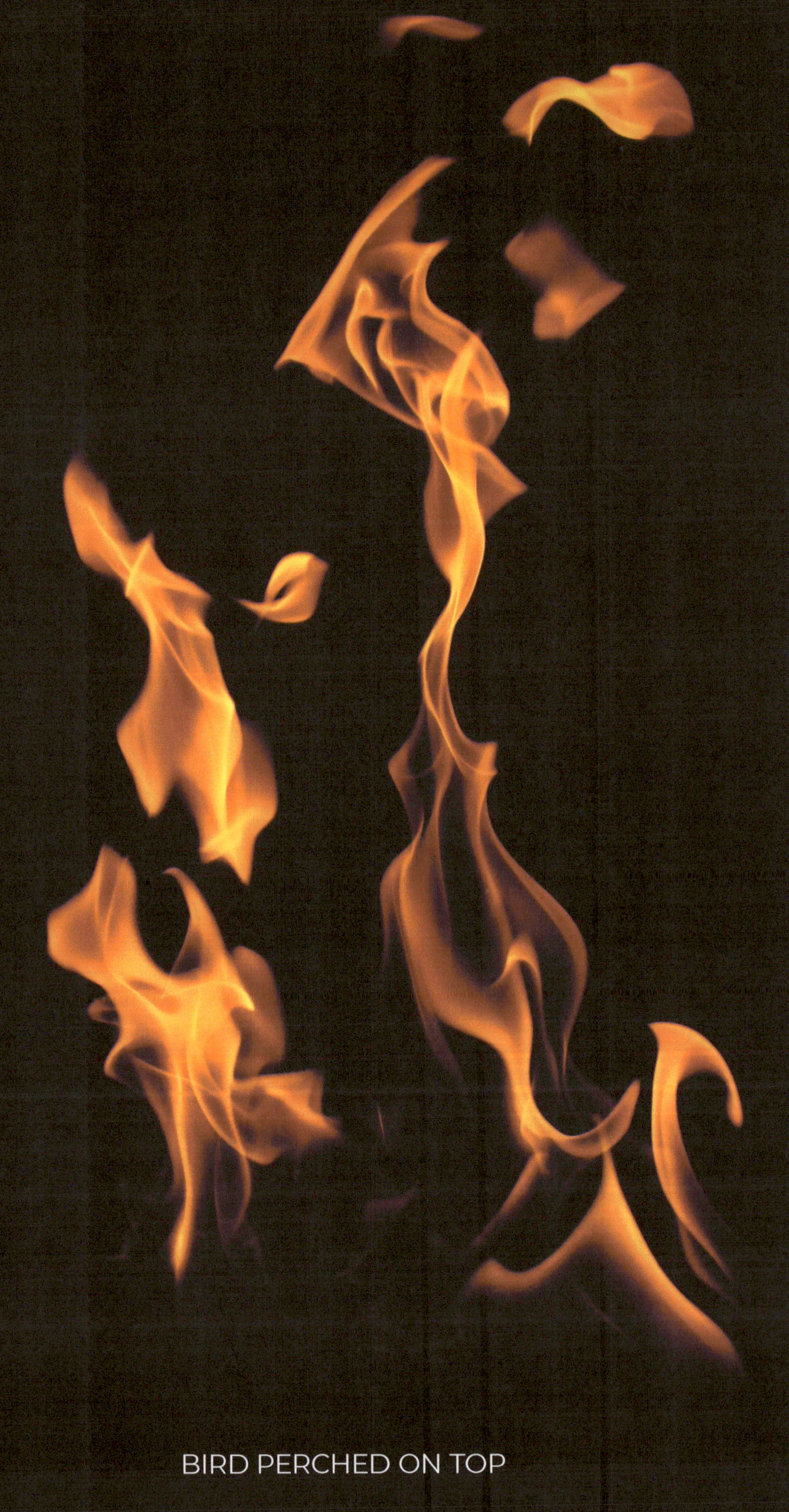

BIRD PERCHED ON TOP

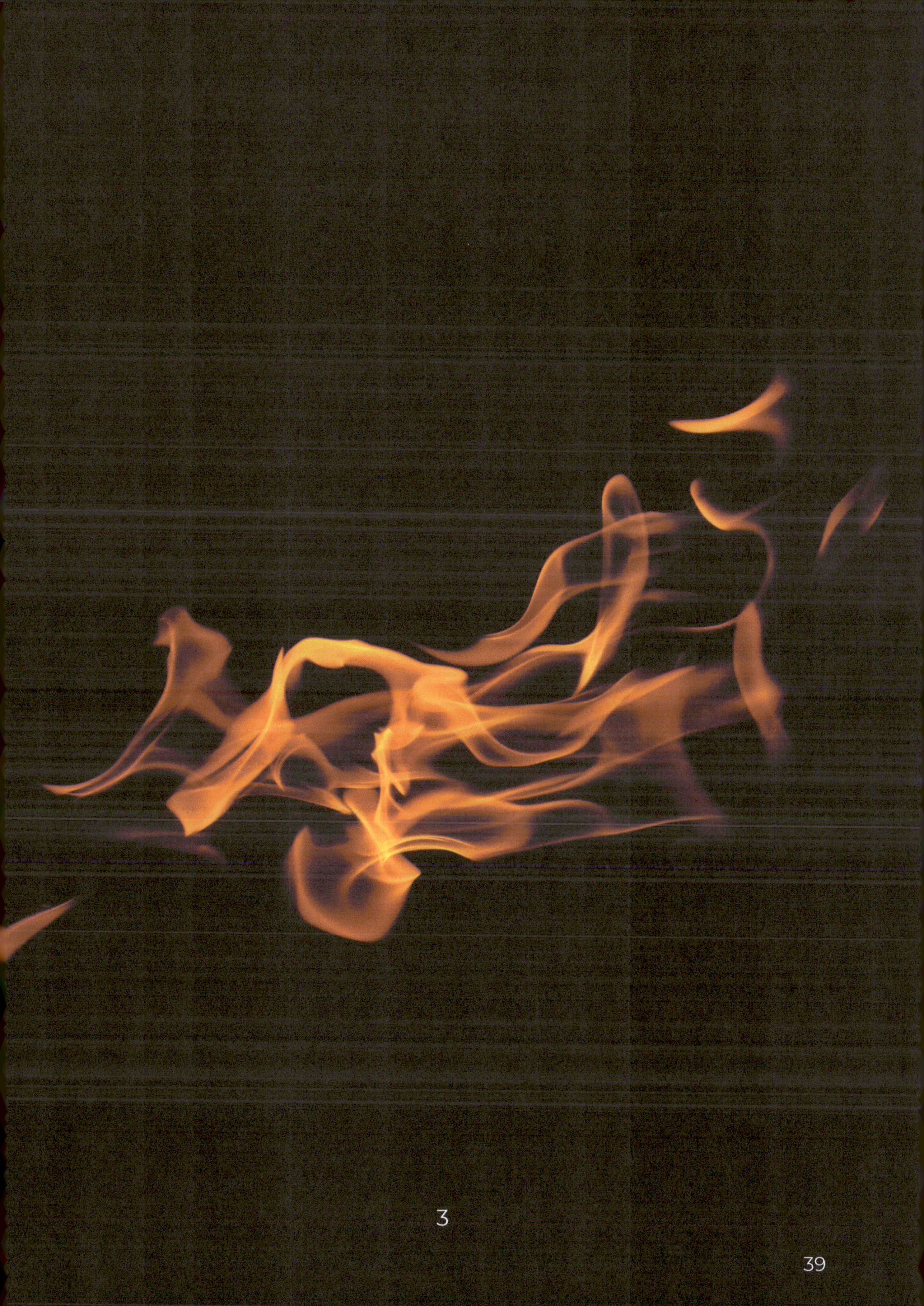

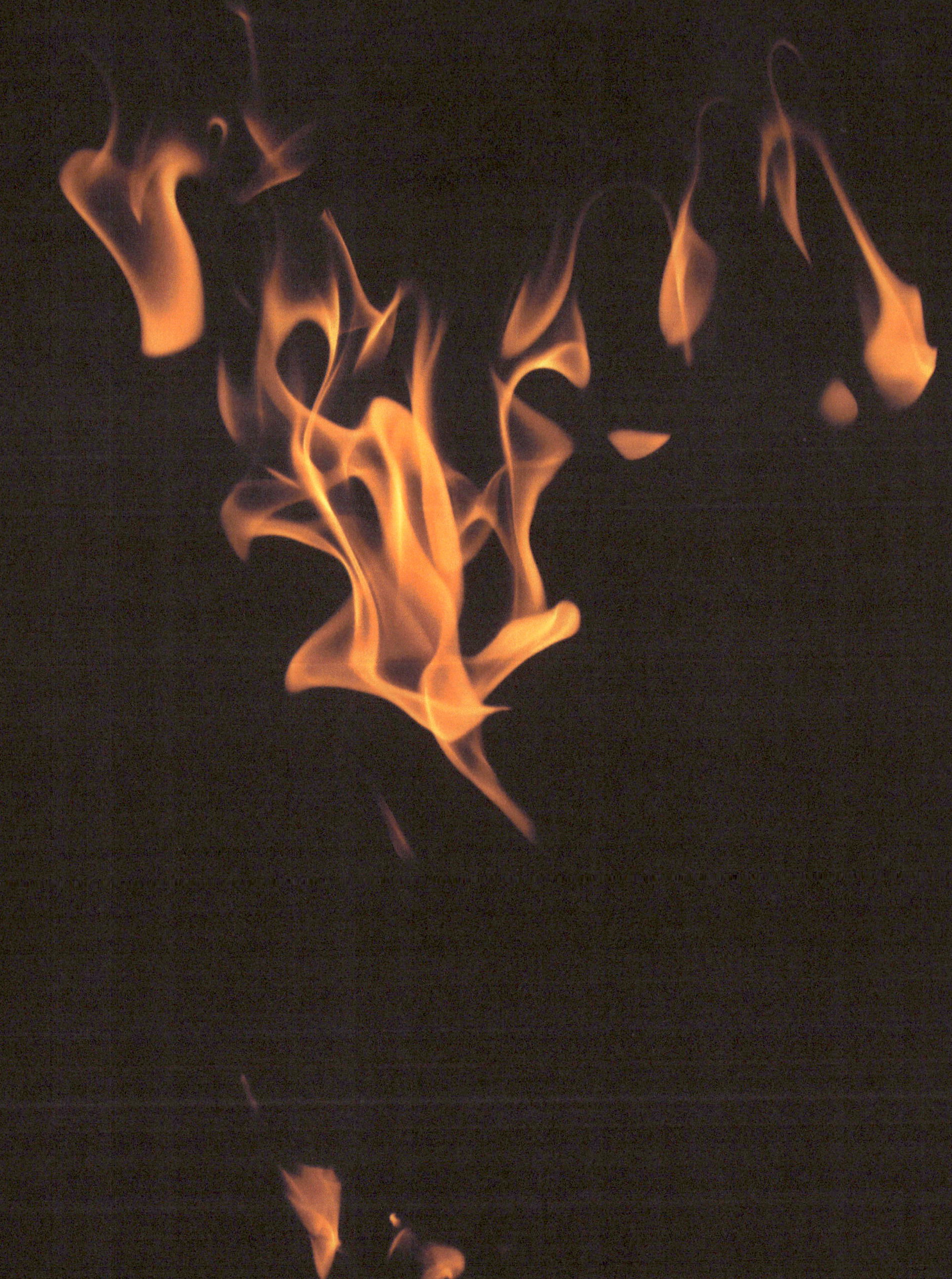

CODED MESSAGE

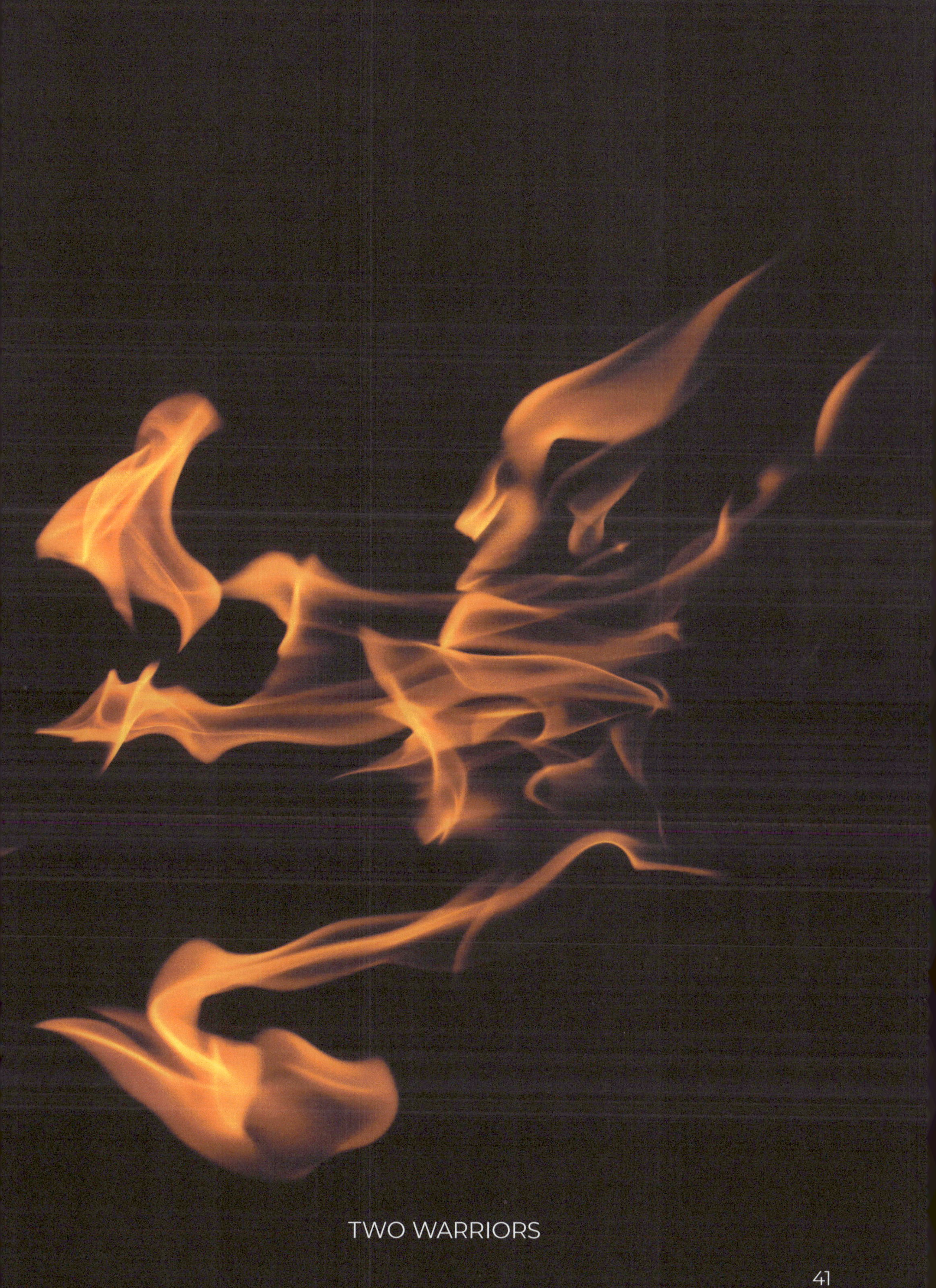

TWO WARRIORS

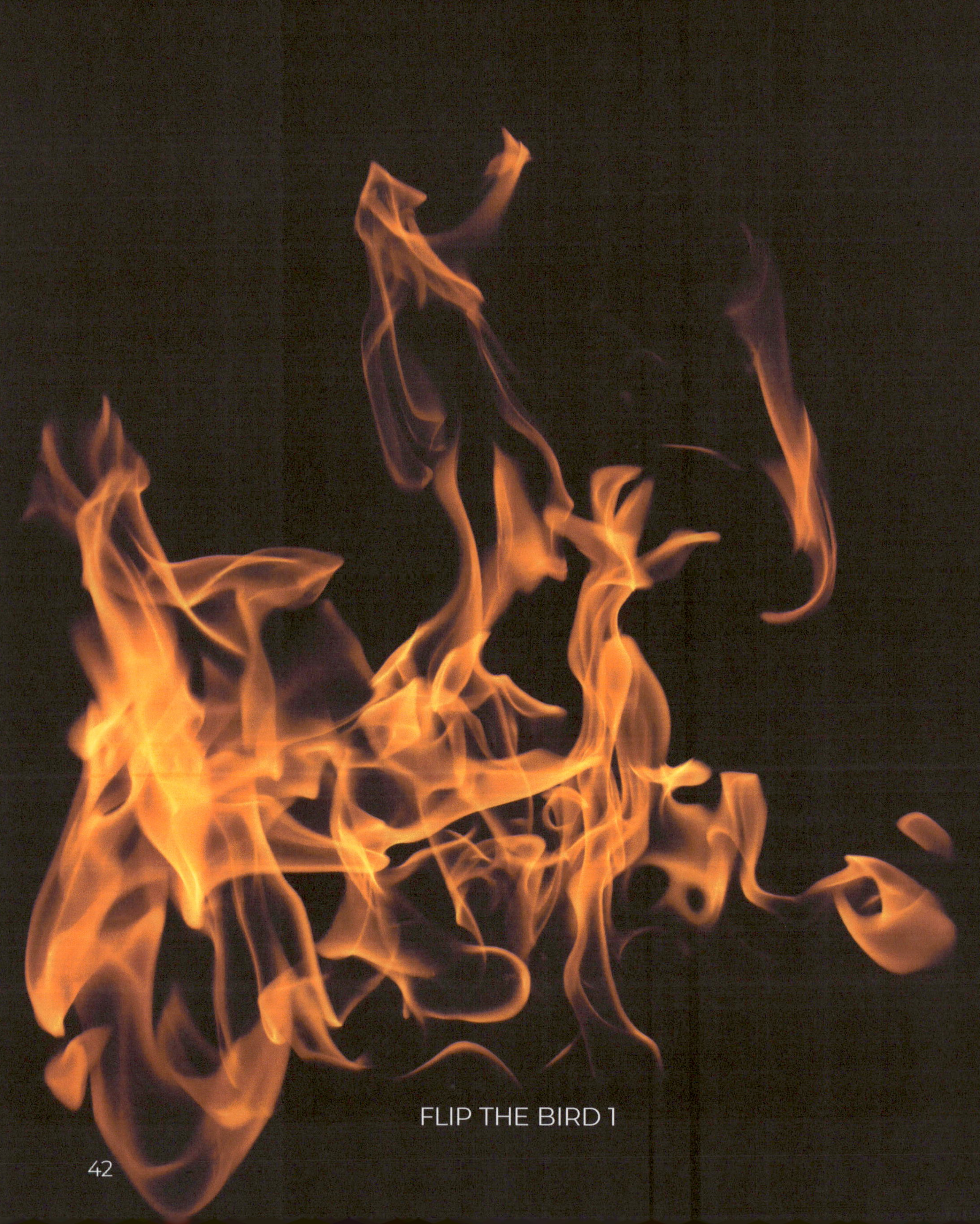

FLIP THE BIRD 1

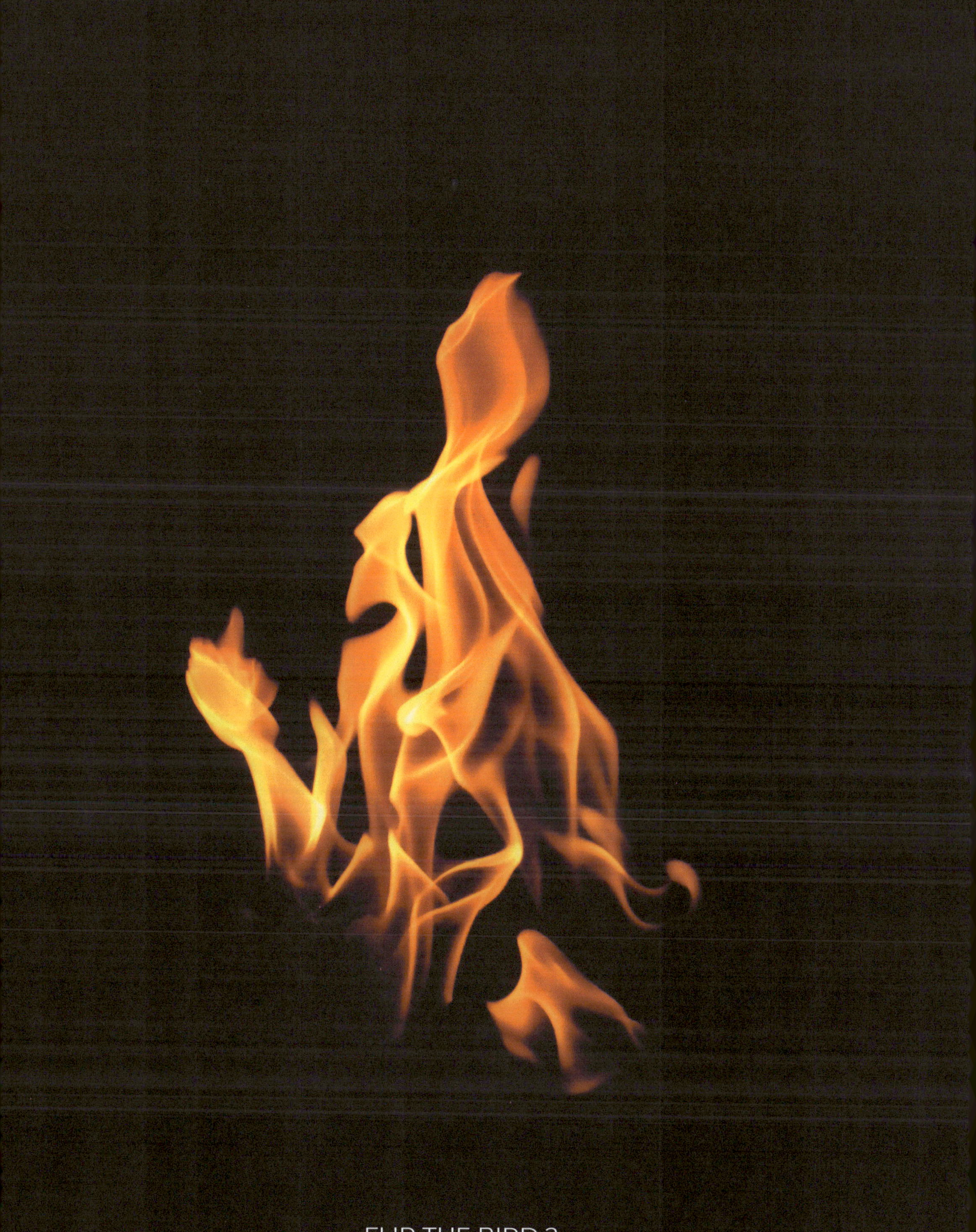

FLIP THE BIRD 2

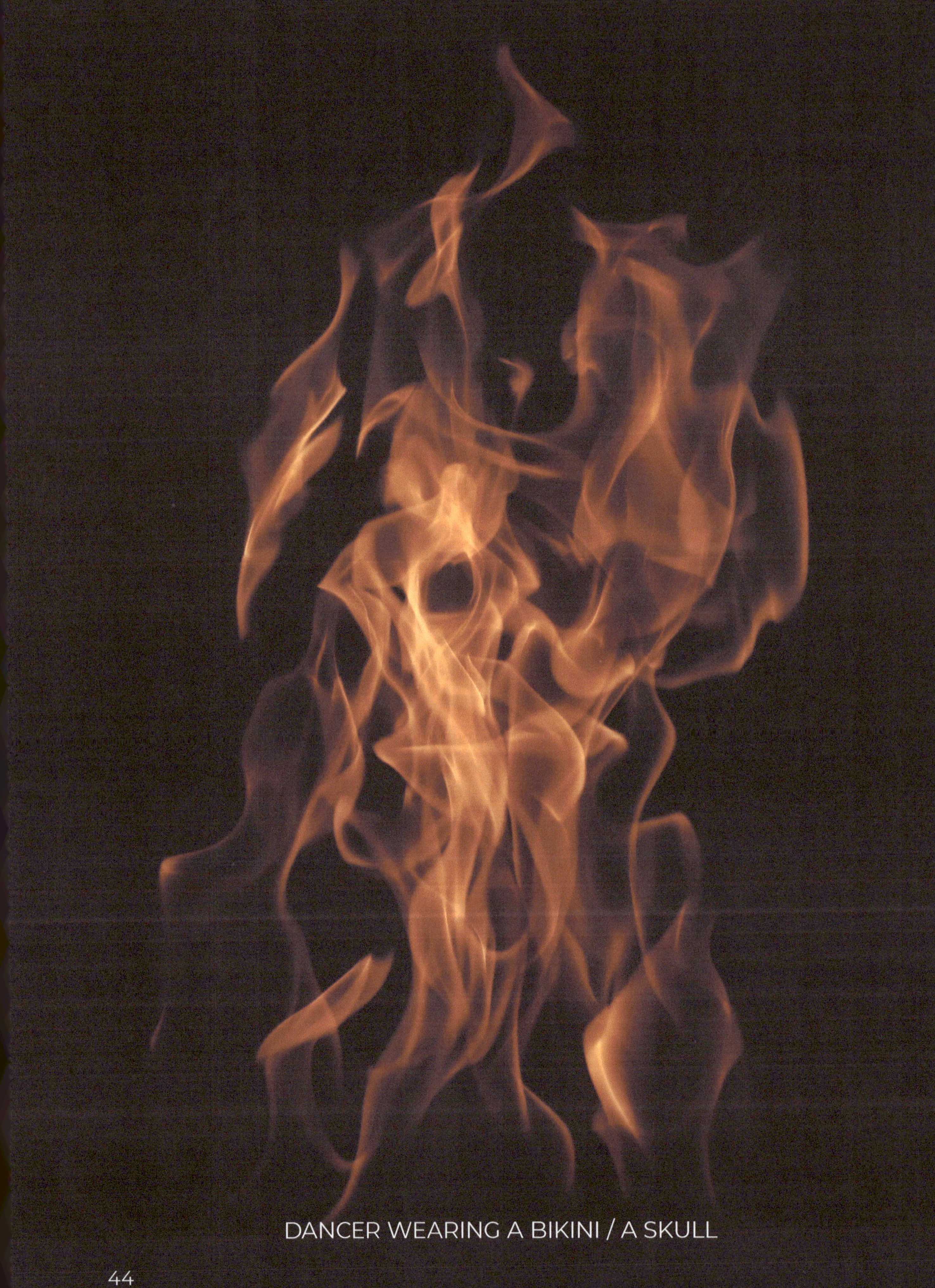

DANCER WEARING A BIKINI / A SKULL

About the Author

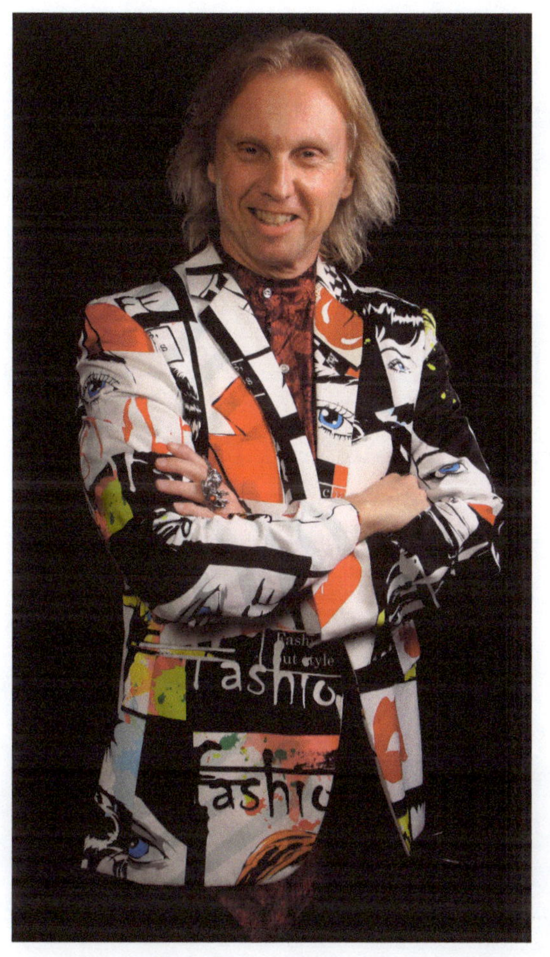

Justyn was born sometime in the last century. He believes that age is just a number and old age only happens if you allow it too. think young, speak young, speak life and not death over yourself and others. The mouth has the power of life and death, so we should use it to create and not to destroy.

He was dropped straight out of heaven and into his mothers womb. Some might even say he landed on his head upon re-entry. If that were not enough at a young age of approximately 6 while riding his bike he flew over the handlebars and landed on his head. Having been knocked unconscious he was carried home by a neighbor friend's parent, Mrs Chambers. the next two days were spent in the hospital with a concussion. A year or two later he would be accidentally hit in the head by a neighbor throwing bricks down the alley. (This may explain why he sees visions, after a few head traumas! JK)

Back in those days he was named John Pratt, by his nine year older brother. Chuck Pratt prayed him into being or existence because he was heavily outnumbered with four sisters. He has two older sisters by the names of Barb and Becky and two younger sisters by the names of Therese and Julie. Justyn is the youngest of the six siblings all born to Rosemary and Charles Pratt. Justyn was told by God to legally change his name, in the spring of 2021. It took him three months to muster the courage to change his name since he knew it was his brother who named him. He knew in his heart that family members would be disappointed or even aggravated by his decision.

But who was he to please, God or man? He chose to be obedient to God and on the day that he went to the court house, upon leaving he photographed a cloud that appeared to be a unicorn in the sky holding a bright and shining diamond upon his outstretched hoof.

Many years prior he was taught by Pastor manuel Ochoa that delayed obedience is disobedience. Justyn is very thankful for the patience of God. God's grace is sufficient for us every day. God grades on the curve of Grace! You see, Justyn had slipped into a deep dark depression after his first born daughter, Linnea Rose died at the age of 26 days. His heart was broken into a million pieces that day. Fifteen years after the death of his first born daughter he would look into the mirror and not recognize himself. He had turned his back on God, his wife Julie Pratt and his three boys Jonathan, David and Noah. their lives had been emotionally turned upside down because their father had chosen selfishness and self centeredness for a time and a season. this situation will be better detailed in the upcoming book "Follow the Signs to your Destiny and Purpose."

The bible says draw close to God and He will draw close to you. That is exactly what Justyn did back in December of 2020. He chose to return to Jesus and ultimately meet God the Father through the love of the Son. The Holy Spirit then began guiding him once more on the journey home, back to his Fathers house. God showed up in his life just in time for him to open his eyes and turn from his wicked ways. Thus becoming a better man, husband, father, brother and friend. The journey home has been one filled with love and laughter as well as sorrow and tears. His heart was being repaired one fragment at a time. Feeling discouraged or sometimes lost on the journey. Justyn would see images first in the air via the clouds, then in the aether. As an avid photographer he began looking up, looking down and looking all around himself. He would then see images in the earth, fire and water. He now has over fifty five thousand images in his collection of The Elements. He has what he refers to as proof of the spirit world working constantly all around us every moment of every day in The Elements. Now two and a half years into the process of drawing close to God, he is healing. Recognizing the darkness within, but choosing the light. Processing the grief, moving through the pain and use of the choices made. He embraced the dark shadows and sat with them for a moment in time. He has learned self love and forgiveness. He has through it all chosen to remain positive, because after all is said and done Positivity is a Super Power! He has leveled up his game and embraced self awareness.

He has chosen obedience to the first and greatest commandment: To love God with your whole heart, mind and soul. The second commandment is to love your neighbor as yourself. God is the artist of Justyn's heart and soul. Justyn is the photographer and artist that God chose to reveal signs and wonders too.

Justyn hopes and prays that you will find peace and love for God, yourself and others on your journey of life.